AGAINST ALL ODDS

WENDY ALEC

Warboys Publishing

Revised edition published 2006 by Warboys Publishing, London, UK

First published 1996 Summit Publishing Limited

A CIP record for this book is available from the British Library.

ISBN–13: 978–0–9552377–2–0
ISBN–10: 0–9552377–2–6

NASB – Scripture quotations taken from the New American Standard
Bible®. Copyright © 1960, 1962, 1963, 1968, 1971, 1972, 1973, 1975,
1977, 1995 by The Lockman Foundation. Used by permission.

AMP – Scripture quotations taken from the Amplified Bible®. Copyright ©
1954, 1958, 1962, 1964, 1965, 1987 by The Lockman Foundation.
Used by permission (www.Lockman.org).

Ch 13: Extract from an article by Peter Popham, used by permission from
The Independent on Sunday.

Production Shirley Ferrier Limited, UK
Cover design Numinos Creative
Typeset by CRB Associates, Reepham, Norfolk, UK
Printed in the United States

CONTENTS

ACKNOWLEDGMENTS

There are very many people who deserve to be acknowledged for their amazing role in the ministry of GOD TV. There are so many to thank that, if we leave anyone out, please forgive us, but know that God the Father sees.

This book is dedicated to all whose names are on this page.

Firstly, to our dear friends, Albert and Pauline Dicken, whose GOD TV story lies within these pages, who have stood with us as visionaries and with this ministry through thick and thin, through hell and high water. Only the Lord can truly repay all that you have done. And only eternity will reveal the spiritual impact in people's lives. We are so *very* grateful to you both for your unfailing love and obedience.

To our stalwart "Scottish intercessor" and treasured trustee, who always wishes to remain nameless. You – who have fought so very very many ferocious battles on our behalf, who has stood through the winds and the storms that have assailed this ministry and never never, not even once, flinched at the onslaught as you have stood in the gap. We love you always. We will meet you on your bridge in heaven. You are God's and our special treasure.

And to James and to "B" who stand alongside you. We are so grateful for their unfailing love and support and prayers. To Jack and Kathleen, Andre and Cliff, we so appreciate your love and prayers.

To Steve Beik – our dedicated and longsuffering "Chief of Staff" – who has stood with us in America through so much warfare and challenging obstacles. You are a true soldier of Christ and we love you from our heart and honor you and Missy.

To Paul Le Druillenac who has been with us "forever"! And

has walked as financial director through some, let us say, "most challenging times"!

To the rest of our executive teams, especially Bo Sanders, our Head of Distribution – we love and honor you and Malin. To our amazing Regional Directors across the world – Thomas Robinson (Asia), Chris Cole (UK), Simon Jacobsen (Scandinavia), Marcel Olivier (Africa). To your wives, so many of whom work shoulder to shoulder with you, supporting you and us and the ministry, Monica, Kerry, Kaja, Caro. We are so grateful to you.

Not forgetting Pauline and Ronnie in our offices in Hong Kong, all our wonderful new American team in our central office in Washington DC, Jeffrey and team in Orlando, Florida, Fergus, Johnny, Klaus, John and Mel and Partner Services and our tireless, multi-skilled production team and all in Angel House, Sunderland, UK, Cecile, Alistair and the communications team in Johannesburg, South Africa, to our amazing creative and vision teams in "AREA 51" in Plymouth, England especially Graeme, Simon, Mick and Charles, to our editors and cameramen and to Peter and our amazing team in Jerusalem, Israel who KEEP us on the air! Our incredible GOD TV teams across the world – You know we always say that GOD TV is like "Saving Private Ryan!"

Without all of you – incredible, faithful, courageous soldiers – the Gospel would not be able to be preached to the uttermost parts of the earth and the battle could not be won!

To all our amazing viewers, especially those who unfailingly PRAY for us – and to our ANGELS who give so tirelessly and generously of their substance.

And lastly to all our wonderful parents, Lona and Stan Perrins, my mother Jean Koefman and to my wonderful father who is in the courts of Heaven praising God Almighty – Doc Koefman.

WE THANK YOU ALL FROM OUR HEARTS.
MAY GOD'S RICHEST BLESSINGS BE YOURS ALWAYS.

ALL the Glory for GOD TV and our media ministry –
for all works past, present and the evangelistic media works still
to come are dedicated to the one to whom all Glory is all due.

To our Glorious heavenly Father, the Almighty God.
Creator of Heaven and Earth.

The LORD reigns, let the earth rejoice;
Let the many islands be glad.
Clouds and thick darkness surround Him;
Righteousness and justice are the foundation
of His throne.
Fire goes before Him
And burns up His adversaries round about.
His lightnings lit up the world;
The earth saw and trembled.

(Psalm 97:1–4 NASB)

HE ALONE IS WORTHY.
HE ALONE RECEIVES THE GLORY.

A SPECIAL WORD TO OUR AMERICAN READERS

There is such an incredible excitement in Rory's and my spirits that keeps growing and growing with each passing day as we hear the whisper of the Holy Spirit saying "There is coming a new move in America."

And as I write this, precious new viewers across the United States, I have to tell you that we are convinced beyond any doubt that in His divine and sovereign purpose God the Father is about to pour out a fresh wave of His anointing across the United States of America.

We feel so privileged that GOD TV can be one of the many vessels that the Father can use as one of the spearheads of this coming revival – as we join with a dread and wonderful army across America in this hour as part of His spiritual Airforce to broadcast His anointing and His person and presence across the airwaves of the USA.

We believe that God is divinely positioning the nations of the United States and Great Britain to align more closely in the Spirit in these coming days, that in the years to come there would be a great joining of the Lion and the Eagle in the spirit realm and as a mighty force of prayer. And that even as there was a winning of the Second World War by this divine aligning in the natural, there shall be a winning of the War of the Last Days by a sovereign spiritual alignment.

As I write these words we humble ourselves under the mighty hand of God in this hour. Our sole and foremost aim in these end-time days is that GOD TV would be a vessel that is pure enough for the Father Himself to pour out His Spirit and His presence to the nations to be a tool of revival and refreshing, of equipping and of sustenance in the perilous days that lie ahead for us on the earth as Christians.

But, back to the United States.

We lived in America in a beautiful old colonial style house on the main street of the wonderful town of Fredericksburg, Virginia for almost three years. Our children went to a wonderful Christian school there and we have to confess we still miss Target, Restoration Hardware, Borders and the steaks and hamburgers at Outback. Our children miss the American Eagle clothes store!

But most of all, we fell in love with your hearts for the Gospel, with your honor of God and His servants and of His word. You are truly a nation of honor. You are a nation of service to God. And if America can be set free from the religious trappings that have so bound her in some quarters, we believe that there is nothing – absolutely NOTHING that God could not do with this nation.

That His desire in this coming season is to thrust America in missions to the nations. That she may fulfill the incredible role destined for her ahead in these last end-time days.

It is our great and awesome privilege to carry men and women of God on GOD TV screens that we believe have a primary role to play in ushering in God's next outpouring across America and the world:

Rick Joyner and Morningstar, Ron Luce and Teenmania, Steve Hill, Kim Clement, John and Lisa Bevere, Rodney Howard-Browne, Francis Frangipane, Tom Hess and the Jerusalem

Prayer Watch, R. T. Kendall, John Paul Jackson, Bob Jones, Derek Prince (his legacy still lives on), Mahesh and Bonnie Chavda, Cindy Jacobs, Mike Bickle and IHOP, John and Carol Arnott, J. John, Steve Schultz and the Elijah List, Patricia King, Lynne Hammond, Liberty Savard, Peter Wagner, Chuck Pierce, Dutch Sheets, John and Paula Sandford, Sunday Adjela, Ken and Lois Gott, Reinhard Bonnke, Hillsong, Colin Dye, Paul Scanlon, Matthew Ashimolowo, Prayer For the Nations, Soul Survivor, Audacious...

The list goes on for pages.

Not forgetting this generation of onscreen generals who have plowed the ground so faithfully that are seen across television screens every day:

Pat Robertson, Benny Hinn, Joyce Meyer, John and Diana Hagee, Kenneth Copeland and T. D. Jakes...

And so very many more. The list is never ending. They have already changed the nation and beyond.

The streams all cross, sometimes they look like juxtaposition but they are all on time in God's divine plan and it is the VERY MIX of these anointings that creates the corporate "THUS SAITH THE LORD" that will literally turn the Body of Christ worldwide.

Many, many of the above ministers are our very good friends and we can only THANK them for their incredible patience over the past four years as GOD TV prepared to launch in the United States at God's sovereign appointed time. Now we are all ready and standing on the brink...

And so – as we begin our early broadcasts into your wonderful nation – precious viewer – know that you have our hearts. Our commitment. Our passion.

Our talents and our gifting we lay at your feet – that the Lord Jesus Christ Himself will break us and our GOD TV team as He broke the bread and fed the thousands – so too says the Lord – *"I will in turn break GOD TV and feed the hungry, the starving, the yearning hearts all across America, that My people may be fed. That My children may be fed. That My eagles may be fed."*

And know that we stand with you, America, in the years to come. That all across the world we may rise as a great and fearsome army in these end times against the works of the devil and to do the works of our Lord Jesus Christ – To glorify the Father and to preach the Gospel of His Son to every nation. Then shall the end come. So be it. Amen.

SELECTED PROPHECIES OVER GOD TV FOR THIS HOUR

Excerpt from prophecy given to Rory and Wendy Alec by Jonathan David in July 1994 at Cornerstone Christian Center, Surrey

I believe very strongly that for both of you, supernatural things are already happening in the heavens.

God shows me that you are like a stone cut out from a different place and God says, *"I have shaped you, I have formed you for a divine purpose but like a stone cut out from a different place, you have tried to fit yourself in so many places that you have found that you are the unfit stone."*

But God brought you here that you might become part of what He is doing here and right across Europe, right across Germany, right across Russia.

And I believe you have, as a couple, a tremendous influence (on the things) that will take place.

People are going to hear about you, even before you ever get on TV.

I don't know if you've been on TV but before you ever do anything, people are going to have their hearts prepared.

I see people even going into the Middle East. This work is going to go even to the Middle East and there is going to be a great reservoir of riches.

But you are going to establish it on a prophetic vein. It's not evangelistic only, it's more than just evangelistic. You're going to establish "Thus saith the Lord."

This network is going to be producing greater miracles by turning entire churches. Entire churches are going to be positioned because of your network.

Your network is not reaching the unreached alone, but it's going to turn the destiny of the Church. It is going to turn the destiny of the Church.

Where you can't go, where ministers can't go, you'll go and the whole Church will turn and when the Church turns you will be a shareholder in everything that breaks forth. You will have spiritual dividends.

Jonathan David had never seen Rory and Wendy Alec before and had no prior knowledge of their involvement in Christian television.

Prophecies given to Rory and Wendy by Cindy Jacobs,
of Generals of Intercession – 1998

The scripture that I get that is foundational for this GOD Network is Isaiah 43:19 – "Behold I do a new thing." And the Lord says, *"I am going to do this new thing,"* And God says to you, *"You are going to have literally stations and studios all over the world for I am raising you up, an apostolic network of television studios from this place."* And the Lord says, *"You will connect the nations of the world together."*

The Lord says, *"I am going to open the door to the United States. I am going to open it wide to you."* And the Lord says, *"I am going to give you favor, I am going to give you favor with a major studio. I am going to give you favor with major studios and networks in New York City. I am going to open a door to New York City that is going to astound you."*

I see New York, Miami and Los Angeles, San Francisco, Chicago, Seattle, Portland, Atlanta.

God says, *"I am going to do it quickly. And there is going to be a whole new generation of leaders, no matter what their age, and they are going to come and they are going to say to you, 'We want this.'"* And the Lord says, *"You will be amazed. You are going to have everything you need."*

There is a great anointing for miracles coming upon the GOD Channel – creative miracles – people that can't see, will see; people tuning in to the program will rise up out of wheelchairs. You have the anointing, Rory and Wendy, and God is going to increase this for the miraculous. You're going to start seeing this as a couple.

And God is going to use the GOD Channel in a major way on the East Coast of the United States. We are seeing destiny take place before our eyes. This is no ordinary time. This is a time of divine visitation, and we are seeing this through GOD TV.

FOREWORDS

1.

This is an exciting book. It even reads in places like a suspense thriller. If one did not believe that this book is based on facts it would seem like a novel that the writer had made up.

This book is Wendy Alec's autobiographical account of how she and her husband Rory brought "GOD TV" into existence. All Christians in the United Kingdom know about GOD TV, but this phenomenon is hardly known in America. Those in Britain who read this book will be amazed at how GOD TV came into being, while those in the United States who read this will be fascinated to know that GOD TV is coming to America.

My own background is Evangelical. I remember reading in *Christianity Today* many years ago that every single Christian television network or station in America was Charismatic rather than Evangelical. The writer of the article wondered why this was true and why Evangelicals had not seized this opportunity. All we know is, the Charismatics got there first and never looked back. They continue to be the dominant factor in Christian television.

There were several things that impressed me about Wendy's book. First, I am sure that GOD TV as it exists today would not have happened had not Rory and Wendy been open to supernatural words of knowledge. In other words, had they been closed to this – like many of us Evangelicals have been – they would have given up many years ago. What kept them going were prophetic words given to them in crucial times that spoke directly to them in the nick of time – just before they were ready to give up. This book should give all Evangelicals pause.

Second, that they were given a mandate to be a ministry of both the Word and the Spirit – that they should broadcast the "uncompromised" Word of God but also report God's move of the Holy Spirit. In short: GOD TV would be Word and Spirit. That has been my own heartbeat for a long time. They wanted GOD TV moreover to be a ministry not a business.

Third, that GOD TV has had severe opposition from the religious world. Not so much from the secular world but the "religious"! When one considers how remote the possibilities have been in getting the Christian message over, you would think that the religious press and religious people would welcome this. But no. GOD TV's keenest opposition has come from those who should have been heralding this opportunity.

I do understand the concern of some that too much of what has been available on Christian television in America would give a wrong impression of Christianity in Europe. Indeed, I myself have been less than happy at the thought of some things I have seen in America would come to Britain! But my knowledge of Church history tells me that you always have the flesh to turn up when God is at work, and that if you are waiting for the work of the Spirit to come in a neat and tidy package one will wait forever! Furthermore, I know of many people who have been converted through programs that sophisticated Evangelicals would dismiss out of hand. My own father-in-law came to the Lord through watching Christian television.

Fourth, Rory and Alec's vision was actually short of what God had in mind! They were thinking only of reaching Great Britain when, along the way, to their astonishment, God let them know He had far more in mind – including Europe, Israel and now America.

This is a story of rags to riches, riches to rags, and back again, of a couple who almost gave up again and again had not God stepped in. I do not think that any unbiased reader of this book will be able to deny that God has raised up this couple in a providential and supernatural way. We used to say in Kentucky that God moves in "mischievous" ways His wonders to perform! You might believe this after reading this book! As for the miraculous, one needs to note that it came with a lot of prayer and hard work as well. It was not a case of passive waiting for God to act.

There are other fringe benefits from reading this. People who pray for their husbands, wives or children to get right with God will find great encouragement to persevere. This book will make you laugh and make you cry, but, most of all, increase your faith that God works on behalf of those who wait for Him.

R. T. Kendall
Former Minister of Westminster Chapel, London (1977–2002)

2.

In every generation, there is a song that rises in the redeemed toward God. It is a hymn of praise, of thanksgiving to God for all He has accomplished in their lives. Yet, added to this, there is a unique song that the end-time saints carry in their hearts. They sing the "song of Moses the bond-servant of God and the song of the Lamb."

Remember, there are many songs sung to the Lamb, yet this is the actual song of the Lamb. It expresses the holy passions of Christ's soul; this song communicated the joy that was set before Him. What is this unique song that Christ, and Moses before Him, sang?

It is the song of nations coming to God!

"Great and marvelous are Your works,
O Lord God, the Almighty;
Righteous and true are Your ways,
King of the nations!
Who will not fear, O Lord, and glorify Your name?
For You alone are holy;
For all the nations will come and worship before You,
For Your righteous acts have been revealed."

(Revelation 15:3–4, NASB)

This passion that "all the nations will come and worship before You" is the song Jesus carried in His heart, even to His crucifixion. Recall the 22nd Psalm, the psalm of the cross. Even as the Lord expressed His suffering and the many astounding prophetic references as He hung dying at Golgotha, He also sung the triumphant closing verses:

"All the ends of the earth will remember and turn to the LORD,
And all the families of the nations will worship before You."

(Psalm 22:27 NASB)

GOD TV, its staff, and in particular Rory and Wendy Alec, its founders, carry this song of the Lamb in their hearts. Their focus is to see "all nations ... come and worship before" God, where every nation hears the gospel and every soul can meet his or her Redeemer.

As Rory and Wendy's pastor, and also as a trustee on their board, I believe the contribution GOD TV is already making to the worldwide Church is significant. But it's about to increase. What I sense goes beyond GOD TV's sparkling creativity and cutting edge innovations; something is coming that is greater than their ability to marry the timeless truths of God with contemporary style and cultures. What I sense pounding – thump-thump, thump-thump – in the soul of GOD TV is the heart of Christ; He's looking at the nations that are opening to His Father. I hear the Song of Moses and of the Lamb, the song of nations coming to God.

Francis Frangipane

INTRODUCTION

This book is dedicated to every Joseph – to every man and woman who has been entrusted with a technicolor dream from God.

You may have been called a young upstart; you may have been thrown in the pit by your "elder brothers" and labeled presumptuous; you may be serving in Potiphar's house, beset by testings, trials and temptations as the Word of the Lord tests you until God's appointed time for you dawns.

You may be serving solitary confinement in the "prison" of circumstances – with "No Way Out" emblazoned all around you in neon letters, surrounded by the barriers of seemingly insurmountable circumstances and obstacles – but take heart, dear dreamer, for on God's appointed day, after all the seeming heartache and disappointments, surely your time will come; and when finally the chief butler remembers you, the gift and calling that God has placed on your life will bring you before Pharaoh just as surely as that other young dreamer before you.

Rory and I had sensed we had a calling on our lives in the area of the media since our early twenties. At a young age we tasted brief success, and then through the next ten years as the Word of the Lord tested us, we were flung onto the Potter's wheel as a loving heavenly Father started to mold and refine His two young dreamers.

In the early years we were the epitome of Joseph sporting his marvelous technicolor coat – brimming with vision and assurance, the Father Himself having given us a multicolored coat of creative talent.

There we were, announcing (like Joseph) in megaphone tones: "*We* have a dream – *we* will affect the nations – *we* will affect the music industry, television and film – millions shall be saved."

And the heavenly Father, in His infinite wisdom, looked at His technicolor clothed visionaries, sighed quietly and said: "It is now time to forge the character integral to the calling that inevitably lies ahead."

And so the vibrant, technicolored robe of a spoilt youngest son grew faded under the harshness of the midday sun, and during the years of toil in the wilderness, the brashness and self-confidence of "I can do it for God" was gently tempered into "God will do it for His Kingdom."

Oh yes, we were thrown into the pit of dashed dreams and broken promises early in our dreamer's walk; we were put to serve under Potiphar in the advertising and television production industry; we were forced to flee from the lust of the eyes, lust of the flesh and the deceitfulness of riches. And when we arrived on the shores of Great Britain, in 1991, we entered our prison years, where it seemed that we were doomed to wander in the wilderness, forgotten, with no sense of direction and set to hard labor with little respite. But our God of fathers after whom every father is named, our God of compassion and mercies, looked down upon His young Joseph – Rory and Wendy Alec – and said, "It is time for THE DREAM!"

And as His young, weary servants moved at His command, He gently washed the dust of the wilderness away from our cheeks and wiped the tears from our eyes. And divinely appointed doors began to open as the Lord God Himself started to pave the way for His young dreamers to launch a Christian television channel that would span all European nations and change the face of religious broadcasting in

Europe. A Christian television ministry that today reaches across the earth's surface, broadcasting from Mount Zion, Jerusalem, on fifteen different satellites in over two hundred nations and territories, reaching over three hundred million people.

Whether you are in the pit, serving in Potiphar's house or languishing in prison – God has a message for you today: "Don't give up: your time will come." For what He has done for Rory and Wendy Alec – through all the seemingly insurmountable obstacles, through all the heartache and disappointment, the laughter and the tears, the mountains and the Red Sea – He will indeed accomplish the same for you.

I pray that as you read these pages the anointing of the Holy Spirit will wash away the dust of discouragement and despair from your mind and heart; that He will revitalize you to fresh hope for the dream that He has placed in *your* heart; that there will be an impartation of the gift of faith, which will strengthen you to face the seemingly impossible circumstances around you, and a super-natural boldness to overcome every demonic assignment and strategy that the enemy has planned to thwart God's dream.

May your heart be comforted, may your soul be encouraged and may the weary arms be strengthened as you walk hand in hand with your Father God until that day when finally *your* time is come and His voice is heard from the heavens: "Call the dreamer – it is *time* for the dream."

Wendy Alec

CHAPTER ONE

ROOTS

I WAS BORN in late January in Welbeck Street in the heart of London, England. As I'm slightly older than Rory I'll indulge in some creative license and omit the year!

My father, fondly called "Doc" by all near and dear, was a physician with a flourishing practice in the heart of London's medical profession – Wimpole Street.

At the outbreak of the Second World War, although based in England, he served as a Captain in the United States American Airforce based in Alconbury, Cambridgeshire, England, where the majority of USA Airbases were.

(My grandfather, Samuel Koefman, was an American citizen. He had been born in Warsaw, Poland, but ran away when he was just fourteen, stowing away on a ship from Riga in Latvia and sailing across the Atlantic to start a brand new life in the United States of America.

He lived and worked for over fifteen years in New York, before sailing to Argentina and then Capetown, where he joined an ox wagon train en route to what was then known as Rhodesia – eventually, in the late 1890s, he settled as an early pioneer in the young city at that time known as Salisbury, where he became a very prosperous businessman. Daddy was born in Salisbury [now Harare] but left to study medicine in Great Britain at the age of eighteen and fell in love with England!)

He served as a doctor in the American bomber division where he was awarded the Presidential Unit Citation when he was wounded on a B17 during the bombing of Dresden.

Daddy always had a great love for America and held dual British and American passports even up until the day he died.

Well, after the war, he set up his medical practice in Wimpole Street, London where he met my mother, Jean. They were made for each other and their marriage was, for nearly fifty years, a wonderful lifelong partnership until his death earlier this year.

Oh, what an incredible man my earthly father was – and when I was born, I was his long-awaited little girl, and he was a gift from God to me even at that early stage of my life.

My mother, Jean, nineteen years younger than my father, was a tough, fiery, practical lady. A born administrator and organizer, she grew up in the hard North of England, in Leeds. She was a fighter with a unique brand of self-sufficiency, having had to fend for herself at a tender age. There was little of the philosopher about the pragmatic young Jean, but then again, my father more than made up for that.

The charming Dr Koefman possessed all the unique qualities that were inherently present in his Jewish heritage. His brilliant academic mind and genteel English manner belied his underlying creative nature, which revealed itself in his life-long love of classical music and art. "All in a day's work" for Daddy meant running his medical practice before studying Russian, playing the violin and reading *The Decline and Fall of the Roman Empire* to unwind.

But the attribute that most affected my young life (apart from his most incredible sense of humor), was the unfailing compassion he displayed to all his patients, regardless of status. There were many nights when he would stay up with a patient who had cancer or who was terminally ill and the next day just look at my mother (who of course looked after the administration of the practice) and gently shake his head, which translated meant, "Don't charge them, Jean."

His only earthbound weakness was a passion for his Jaguar cars, which he did indulge in for most of my childhood years, but Daddy had long learned that to give meant to receive.

So there I was – a typical British doctor's daughter and no doubt fairly spoiled! "Daddy's girl." I was educated in a private school in Surrey, where I learned the violin, took ballet and singing and was taken to West End first nights of opera, ballet and theatre, all from the age of four. My younger brother had entered this scenario when I was two and from all accounts, I was not particularly amused. God bless you, Robert!

Then, at the age of eight, destiny entered and my parents made a decision to emigrate to South Africa. God, in His divine overview, ensured that this little English girl landed in Durban, South Africa – a whole continent away – and so a new life began.

I was enrolled in an all-girls Catholic convent presided over by German nuns, as my parents felt that this offered the best academic standard.

My parents were extremely strict (especially my mother) and were insistent on high grades and good behavior. Up until the age of thirteen, I was the most disciplined, conscientious, hardworking and well-behaved student in class. But the term that High School began, the decay set in or, as my parents said, "Teenagitis" began.

My schoolwork deteriorated as I started to gravitate more and more towards Speech and Drama and Music. This did not bode well for a child who was being groomed by her parents to be a doctor. As High School progressed, I became the class clown and rebel. I was cheeky, incredibly strong-minded and started to buck authority. I was late for classes. My middle name was "trouble."

In my final year I behaved so badly that I was demoted as a prefect and sat languishing in detention, much to my conservative parents' horror. This was not how a "doctor's daughter" should behave!

But during all my rebellious teenage years I was hungry for God. At the age of eleven I had been to a school mass at the Catholic convent where the priest had held up a picture of Jesus and the Sacred Heart. In my heart, always longing after God, I had said: "God, if you give each of us a picture, I will *know* that You love me and I will be Yours for ever." Although there were several hundred of us there, each one of us was given a picture of Jesus . . . and I never forgot this act of God.

The next year, Billy Graham came out to Durban. I went up in the altar call. My heart longed for God and with a childlike faith I committed my life to Jesus . . . but I had *no* teaching. I didn't understand salvation.

After matriculating from the convent, I was enrolled at Natal University in Durban. My behavior went from bad to worse. I was sleeping late, skipping lectures, tanning on the beach or on the balcony all day and then partying at night. And this was *every* night, till four or five in the morning.

There was something in my nature that needed to thrive on risk. Risk in relationships, in habits, in lifestyle . . . and it started to take its toll. My parents received a letter from the Dean of the University, which actually stated, "We despair of Wendy's behavior."

Needless to say, due to too much partying and no work, I failed my second year of university. My normally calm and self-controlled British father excommunicated me from the family! To him, I was as dead. I did not exist.

I was a month short of my eighteenth birthday.

Things went further downhill and I degenerated into the night-club and music scene with my "degenerate" cronies. We danced till four in the morning and rose at one every afternoon, did our hair and make-up – and went on the town. EVERY night. I was mixing primarily with long-haired male musicians and music producers, and was involved in several relationships at once. They would buy me my cigarettes, take me to dinner and encourage my song-writing career. I was acting just like a bimbo and lapping it up avidly. I didn't care who was hurt. All I cared about was gratification for the moment and I loved it. The pretty wild music producer I was involved with at the time formed a music group for me, and I and my "boy band" called "First Offence" started serious rehearsals on my repertoire of songs.

(Take hope for all your wayward teenagers, parents.) I was so wild that the local charismatic church found me two nice, unsuspecting Christian families to try and bring me into some order. Neither of them succeeded in "taming" me as I drove both families up the wall by continually breaking out at night to be with boyfriends.

I was now enrolled at drama college and staying in a girl's youth hostel. And now my "new" boyfriend, another music producer, had set up a serious gig engagement for my new band at "Whispers", one of Durban's more serious clubbing venues. This was moving onward and upward in the secular music world – but downward away from anything to do with God. It was a really bad, *bad* scene.

The end of the year found me finishing off a pop set in a night club and then singing the oldie "Cocaine" by J. J. Cale when one of the more "conservative", strait-laced Christians, who was deeply concerned about me, having heard about my secular antics, came to seek me out.

Being by nature dramatic and creative, I had always felt that I could never fit into this strict and virtuous Christian mold.

"Ms Strait-lace" (looking like a Pear's soap advert) cornered me in the ladies' room, where I glared at her grimly from over my cigarette holder holding my black "Sobrani" cigarette! (looking like a more dubious kind of ad!) and with tears brimming over, she confronted me: "What are you doing to Jesus?"

An intense anger rose within me. I wanted to lash out at her. (How grateful I am for her obedience – that she cared enough to follow me into the club that night. It revolutionized my destiny.) She finally left and I was alone facing my reflection. Suddenly, the room was filled, saturated with the presence of Almighty God. Very slowly, I looked up into the mirror and I saw the Lord Jesus Christ. I remember instinctively wanting to run away, thinking He was going to be so angry with me because my life was in such a mess.

But you know, Jesus looked at me and oh, how He loved me. Through all the years that have passed, I have never forgotten that moment.

It was His eyes. They were filled with such tender mercy and compassion. His eyes literally blazed with a passion and a love for me ... and all the while, tears were running down His face.

Instead of judgment and condemnation, the Lord Jesus was crying for me. In that split second I discovered a love that would fill the vacuum inside me that I'd been trying so desperately to fill with relationships, highs and challenges.

I finally surrendered my life to the Lord Jesus Christ ... and it was completely turned around in an instant. Wild as I had been, my life was transformed and revival started to sweep through my dormitory of very rebellious friends at the hostel.

The only people who remained *completely* unconvinced by my dramatic conversion were the tight-knit group of Christians – the "Pharisees and Sadducees" on the next floor – who proceeded to stare at me on occasions in the lift with that severe "whitewashed sepulchered" glare, because they knew that I was holding Bible studies while I was still smoking!

In fact, I would read the Bible while my precious band of worldly rebels would sit in all kinds of confrontational, defiant positions listening to the Word of God. But you know, many, *many* of them came through to the Lord!

How grateful I am that God doesn't judge people on the outside. In the Amplified translation, it says that Jesus ate with the *pre-eminently* wicked and oh – how I love that. That is why on some of GOD TV's earlier publicity (as in our advert in the *Sky* magazine we wrote – "GOD'S NOT IN A BOX – HE'S ON THE BOX!")

Oh – how much God loves *all* people. He's not as concerned with the externals as most of us tend to be. He bypasses that and goes straight to the heart.

Now remember, I'm not condoning smoking. I'm saying that God deals with all of us in different ways at different times, and when our hearts are truly surrendered to Him and we grow in the Word of God, the externals will come into line with the change in our spirit and soul. God majors on the inside, not the externals ... *always*.

And so, an intense desire was birthed in my heart to reach the "real" world – the secular world – people who found it hard to relate to "church" and "religion." I already sensed deeply – at this very early stage of my Christian walk – that one of the most powerful ways to achieve this was through music and drama (the only media tools I knew or understood at the time).

A few weeks later, I found myself seated in front of the Pastor's wife of Durban Christian Center. (I still looked more as if I had been dragged out of the nearest smoke-filled club, dressed in my tight black leather outfit, than having an appointment with a pastor's wife!) How gracious that lady was to me. There I was, stubbing out cigarette after cigarette into her rubbish bin, and there she was, just loving me with the love of Jesus.

Well, she just loved me ... and then she prophesied. That was over twenty years ago – and these words from the prophecy were branded in my soul.

> *"And you shall be raised up as a forerunner*
> *of creative evangelism in this generation."*

And so, I started on a collision course with God's destiny for my life. And in the years to come, God was to train up both Rory and me and open our eyes to what I believe to be one of the most powerful evangelistic tools in these last days – the Media.

CHAPTER TWO

ENTER RORY

IN JANUARY 1981 I enrolled in a discipleship training course at Youth With A Mission in Scotland (they made us smoke outside in the snow!) and went on to join a church in Sussex (and *finally* stopped smoking!)

In the winter of 1982 I returned to South Africa to enroll at Rhema Bible College in Johannesburg. And oh – what precious years followed. The next five years were what I call my "wonder years," a time when I was privileged to be totally set apart and separated to the Lord.

For months I was able to lock myself away and spend hour after hour alone with the Holy Spirit. Many afternoons I would be found face down at the back of Rhema Bible Church, interceding, in between following up new coverts from the Sunday services and counseling people with needs. I was also involved with a multi-racial singing group traveling around South Africa, praying for the sick and ministering in a very young, prophetic anointing.

Sometimes, I have to confess, in the hectic, pressurized lifestyle of the GOD Channel, I look back longingly on those wonder years!

The angels were no doubt working hard, for one weekend in God's blueprint – I was invited to minister at a church in the small mining town of Rustenburg.

"I don't want to go to Rustenburg!" I stated to my longstanding friend, Annie Chikwase who now runs "Kondanani", looking after Aids orphans in Malawi.

She looked at me with the glint of God in her eye.

"You *need* to go."

I arrived at the morning service and there, leading the praise and worship, was a vibrant young man who played the keyboards in a manner that immediately got my attention. Music was still my passion.

This talented young man was Rory Alec.

Rory was born Rory Alec Stephen in the small mining town of Rustenburg, South Africa.

His mother, Lona, at twenty-two was an unusual, independent young woman, who had been estranged from Rory's natural father, Robert Stephen, even before his birth.

After the marriage breakdown, when Rory was just a few months old, Lona moved to Durban to continue her career as a radiographer. Rory, blissfully unaware of the emotional break-up, was looked after in the hospital nursery. The family's memories are of a contented, adaptable, sunny infant adored by young and old alike.

When Rory was one he gained a new stepfather, Paul Jordaan – a genuine, kind man. Almost straight away a brother and a sister were born. Deep down Rory started to feel that he was the outsider. Unfortunately, after only a short time of marriage, there was an amicable separation. Rory was just five years old.

Lona and the children moved back up to Rustenburg where her

father owned a farm, the scene of many memorable childhood weekends. But it was at the local hospital that Lona's destiny was about to change forever.

Stanley Perrins, a newly qualified physiotherapist, had just arrived to take up a post at the local hospital in Rustenburg. Suffering from a degenerative eye disease, he was already 80 percent blind. Stan was one of those rare finds in today's society – solid gold. His keen mind was coupled with a code of unparalleled integrity and honor. Stan was unflappable, perceptive and literally the salt of the earth! Although Lona was not by *any* means interested in any relationship, they became friends and in 1972, when Rory was eight, they were married. Rory, having had no contact with his natural father, was adopted by Stan and everyone finally settled down into a stable family life.

School was basically a non-event for Rory. He was not by any means an academic and preferred to spend his leisure time involved in music, which had been his passion since boyhood. His mother, sensing her son's natural musical aptitude, invested in an organ and Rory began music lessons. By the age of fourteen, he was playing the piano and keyboards, drums, guitars – literally anything that made a sound! It was an unusual musical gift, and in time it would start to open doors in the South African music and advertising industry. But for the meantime, school was to be endured.

Then teenagehood struck with a vengeance.

Rory was *far* more conservative than I and never had my tendency to kick over the traces. He found himself facing a different form of temptation.

A clash of wills arose in the household between stepfather Stan and the young Rory. The sound of harsh words, slamming doors and flaring tempers raged day after day for months on end.

During this volatile and emotionally unstable period of home life, Rory found himself profoundly impressed by a new exchange

33

student at school, Warren Edminster. Warren always seemed calm and unruffled by circumstances around him. However, he approached Rory for advice about his girlfriend problems and Rory, in turn, started to ask some leading questions about this "born-again thing." They got together for a lunch of burgers and milkshakes. Rory dealt with the girlfriend problems in five minutes then listened to Warren witness to him for the rest of the afternoon.

Rory ended up one evening in a prayer meeting led by Andre and Cliff Scott. At the end of the evening, Andre sensed strongly that a young person wanted to give their heart to the Lord Jesus and asked if they would please raise their hand. Rory, to his initial dismay, found that his hand had gone up.

That evening in a small house group, surrounded by the love of Jesus, Rory prayed the sinner's prayer from his heart, and committed his life to Jesus.

The next day at school, after hearing what had happened to him, Rory's friends started to mock him, saying, "So, now you're an angel," but by the end of the day, they had become intrigued by the unmistakable change in his language and behavior. Victor, one of Rory's friends, proceeded to give his life to Jesus and needless to say, many others in Rory's school were born again.

And two years after his conversion, I arrived at the church in Rustenburg ... and there was Rory leading praise and worship!

Now, Rory was still serving in the South African Defense Force and had this remarkably short haircut. I had always been attracted to guys with *long* hair. So Rory immediately had a strike against him, courtesy of the Armed Forces.

But Rory started to call me and he didn't stop calling. The fact that he was also a brilliant musician made it extremely difficult for me to ignore him. (Actually he was very cute!)

Then the pastor's wife dropped a bombshell.

"Oh," she said casually, "Rory believes that God has said that you're to be his wife!"

In fact Rory had gone to his pastor the day before I arrived and said that God had said that he would meet his wife the next day. I have to admit that I *did* get a fright at this unexpected comment, as Rory was younger than I was.

But, by this time, we had got a Christian musical group together and were faithfully driving the neighbors and Rory's parents near to dementia by practicing the entire rock opera repertoire every weekend.

And so, praise the Lord, Rory eventually finished his army service and grew his hair (very long, actually) – much to my conservative mother's horror.

God had brought together two young Christians, who loved each other and the Lord Jesus with all their hearts, with a vision to reach out to the world through creative evangelism. Actually, I must qualify that . . . an *enormous* vision.

You see, the one thing that Rory and I never queried, even at such a young stage of our relationship, was the fact that God had called us to affect nations and that the calling on our lives would change the world. There was never a flicker of doubt in our minds. Even at that infantile stage, God had said the vision would go from South Africa to the United Kingdom and eventually to the *United States*.

And as we grew in the Word through the years, it became evident that this absolute assurance and conviction that God could use us as "little David" to impact the media (Goliath) was actually the gift of faith in operation.

And we both had a strong but unchanging sensing in our spirits that this destiny for us was to start in the United Kingdom.

A few months later, Rory was discharged from the army after successfully completing two years of military service. Earlier that year, he had received seven thousand rands ($700) from an inherit-ance. Without hesitation, he invested it in the recording of the title track from the rock opera, *We Want Our Money Back*. It was time to go public.

In grand style, we embarked on what would be the norm in our later careers and calling – a Presentation Evening, to share the vision with hopefully wide-eyed onlookers who would catch it.

A friend of ours in catering, enthused by the vision of the rock opera, donated the use of his restaurant for the evening, which we packed out with every friend, relative, relatives' friend and any other rather unsuspecting guest who had most probably been lured there by the promise of a decent meal, rather than because of our supposedly budding talent!

Let me mention here that by this time Rory had been reunited with his natural father and a profound reconciliation had taken place. So that evening, Bob Stephen was one of our special guests.

Well, the lights were dimmed and the sound went on (extremely loudly) – we had the audio in those days but lacked the visual. The parents looked very proud, the friends were excited (if they didn't they wouldn't get dinner), and the secular record company represent-ative stared round in a state of unease, if not alarm. (He *had* been warned it was a Christian event.)

However, the evening ran its course and the previously extremely hungry and very bored "Christian lady" (who was known to raise inordinately large sums of money for secular film projects) suddenly had a mood swing. Her eyes started to sparkle with what we desperately hoped was the recognition of "raw" talent...

So much did her eyes shine, that within a few months, several million rands had been raised for three Gospel musical projects, one of which was ours and we were paid fifteen thousand rands ($1,500) just to appear in our own music video.

To cut a long story short, we became engaged and were married on January 10, 1987 in Durban. We honeymooned in South Africa and were flown to the south of France immediately afterwards to attend MIDEM, Europe's most prestigious music festival. There followed five-star hotels in Nice and Cannes ... posters, presentation packs ... next stop, London, pocket money, dinners and a quick indoctrination into London's West End to prepare us for our project to come. We saw *Time, Cats, Les Miserables, Me and My Girl, Starlight Express, Chess* and *Phantom of the Opera*. Rory had just turned twenty-one – the rising Christian media evangelists were on course and about to learn some *valuable* lessons.

On our arrival back in Johannesburg, we went straight into the music studio to start working on the full rock opera album. Rory and I wrote the music, I wrote the lyrics and Rory and Nikki Saks arranged the musical tracks.

During the next three months, however, the music projects changed in the producers' minds from Ministry to Business ... and oh, what a subtle but dangerous shift this was. Strife between the producers set in and within a few weeks the project disintegrated, with many question marks as to their misappropriation of funds.

And so, Rory and I and two other artists were left as the unsuspecting Christian artists in a shambles of broken promises and commitments, lawyers and accountants.

We were so grieved that greed and selfish ambition had destroyed the birthing of what we believed to be potentially one of the most progressive and far-reaching Christian media projects of the eighties.

But in the maze of shattered dreams, Father God comforted us, saying – "This is where you're *going* ... now I'm going to help you to grow up and train you up." And God started to put us through His own training process to build the character and steadfastness that surely was integral to all that would lie in wait for us.

Desperate to continue to generate a living, we burst our way into the life of one of South Africa's best-loved secular comedians – Eddie Eckstein (the South African equivalent of the British Lenny Henry). Eddie had a bunch of midi-gear (musical recording equipment) standing amongst his comedy library and research material in the cellar under his house.

"We'll make it work for you, Eddie!" we enthused. And with Eddie an aghast onlooker, we proceeded to turn the bits and pieces into a workable studio.

Our career in the secular media gingerly lurched forward. And although we didn't understand why God would seemingly place us in the secular media world, when we so desperately wanted to be involved in Christian projects, God in His magnificent overview was starting to train us up for the future.

We started out by selling our wares to the cut-throat advertising industry. Within a couple of months, we were regularly writing music and lyrics for the ad agencies. Commissioned to write radio jingles for them, we produced material for corporate launches and cabaret shows.

One morning during this period, twenty-two-year-old Rory had a bright idea in the bath. South Africa had suffered severe floods. With visions of Bob Geldof floating on the horizon, he uttered – "Let's create a flood album."

And they did. Eddie and Rory became executive producers on one of South Africa's most remarkable projects. Two long-playing record albums were launched in aid of the 1988 South African disaster fund. Rory and Eddie organized a major campaign to promote the sale of the flood albums and coordinated sixty-four companies from all over South Africa to sponsor the entire campaign.

Soon after that, one of our most loyal clients approached us, offering us a wonderful remuneration package if we would only come and work for their agency.

Our advertising career began.

Rory became agency radio producer, and I became copywriter. God took us from concentrating on just the musical gifting that He had placed in us and started to expand our creative talents in a *very* secular world.

God looked on us with great favor and we were soon promoted to middle management, working on national campaigns across South Africa for clients such as French Connection/Jordache, National Panasonic and Pizza Hut, learning the vital aspects of combining USPs (Unique Selling Points) with highly creative concepts to gain universal appeal.

Then came the introduction of television in the form of the production of agency television commercials. God, as He prepared us, started to marry audio and visual together, preparing us for the mammoth tasks ahead.

But God's vision for the media still burned in our hearts. We sensed that God had called us to an apostolic, prophetic media ministry – encompassing television, film and music – that would not only affect the Christian world, but would have a major impact on everyone else.

It was during this time in advertising after the heartache of the Christian music project that we cried out to God, "Father, confirm our calling. Give us a sign that You have indeed called us to affect the face of the media in this generation."

Almost immediately, we received a phone call from South Africa's equivalent of the BBC, the SABC (South African Broadcasting Corporation) saying that the music video from our rock opera produced from the Christian music project had been nominated in the secular Telefunken Top Music Video of the Year Awards. (We hadn't even known that it had been entered.)

This was like being nominated for a Christian song on the UK *Top of the Pops*. A one in a million!

We arrived at the SABC studios on the day of the awards with no record company, no agent or manager amidst all the heavyweight secular groups and their heavyweight entourages.

And when the winner was announced, it was ... "Rory Alec for 'Mr X'!"

The press had a field-day with the headline: "Unknown wins top music award." We won fifteen thousand rands ($1,500).

Once again, God had confirmed our calling in the midst of the "unbelievers." What constantly seemed to distinguish us from those around us involved in "church media" was the fact that the acclaim or recognition for the giftings in our lives was coming from the "world" rather than from the Church.

A year later, the agency broke their profit share arrangement with us and we were led, we believe now, by the Holy Spirit, into the wilderness of the television commercial production industry, to be tempted by the devil.

CHAPTER THREE

THE POWER AND THE GLORY

IT WAS NOW the end of 1988. We were still faithfully attending Rhema Bible Church in Johannesburg with the vision for the media and Britain burning like a flame in our hearts.

At every invitation for those called to full-time ministry, Rory and I would zealously rush up to the front of the church. But for all our commitment to God to be used in Christian media and move to the United Kingdom, the doors continued to open for us in the secular media industry in South Africa. We would have to be patient and wait for God's perfect timing.

Now it was time for us to enter the cut-throat, dog-eat-dog world of cinema and television commercial production, where only the fittest or the most capitalized survive.

When we launched Alec-Gene Productions (our television commercial production house), there were about a hundred production houses servicing the sophisticated advertising industry in

Johannesburg. Approximately ten to twelve of these could be termed major players.

We started at position number one hundred and one and by the time we hit our *glorious* demise, we had successfully hyped, busked and marketed ourselves into the Top Ten.

To succeed in the highly competitive industry of television commercial production, we needed either a film director who could rank with the best, as we had to "pitch" for commercial work, or we needed an inordinate amount of chutzpah!

Needless to say, we had the latter.

The entrepreneur in each of us raced ahead in our zest to conquer the South African advertising industry and Sandton, the mecca of Johannesburg's major advertising agencies, was the place to be. In our finite minds, we decided that *obviously* God was going to raise Alec-Gene Productions as a beacon of light in the industry. We would then open a London branch and so – we (Joseph with the megaphone) would finance Christian media projects.

All nice and cosy and comfortable: this plan completely eradicated the looming possibility that we might have to go to London by faith. Lord, preserve us! Ours was a much better plan. We would make a couple of hundred thousand rands, preferably more, and then relocate to London (to take over the film industry, naturally!).

And so ... with this logic in mind, and believing that God was with Alec-Gene Productions, we flexed our empire-building muscles and burst forth onto the unsuspecting tight-knit, cynical, arrogant production industry.

To fill you in, cinema and television commercial production in Johannesburg was basically the "yuppie" side of television. In comparison with production for the state-owned television (SABC) and the relatively infantile film industry in South Africa, serious television commercial production involved putting a huge amount of money, time and co-ordination into thirty seconds' worth of product.

Many of South Africa's commercials were recognized at both the highly prestigious British and American commercial awards.

It was an industry filled with ambitious, upwardly mobile, highly talented and grossly overpaid film directors and producers. (Many were on cocaine, with expense accounts in the stylish Sandton restaurants that matched the expense-leased sports cars they drove.) And they all had one overriding ambition – to *make* it.

In late 1988 we joined the ranks of the Perrier-sipping, Gucci-clad, Sandton commercial crowd to make our mark. Commercials had to be "won" from the advertising agency. We immediately descended on the fifty-two advertising agencies to "pitch" for work, with what we considered to be an inspirational marketing idea.

Our production secretary was an ex-make-up artist. So I had her fill fifty-two glass vials with make-up blood and place them on cotton wool in small glossy black boxes with the label – "FRESH BLOOD IN THE MARKET-PLACE."

Apart from the reaction of a few paranoid creative directors (who thought the blood was a death threat), where other production companies had labored for years to become known, we achieved instant recognition in the advertising agency arena. All eyes were suddenly glued to this young, upstart production house.

This was combined with a wild report that Rhema and Pastor Ray McCauley were financing the production house. (Not true!) Word now spread like wildfire in Johannesburg's advertising industry that "the *Christians*" were among the heathen.

Now we were confronted with our first challenge – the advertising agencies admired our innovation and flair, but would our film production be good enough for them to entrust us with our first commercial?

Enter Nik, a young creative music video director and a talented but volatile free spirit. He would work for us but refused to sign anything contractually. Having already painstakingly gone through what felt like hundreds of uninspiring young director's showreels, we reluctantly agreed to these terms, believing that there was enough raw talent in Nik to get the agencies' attention.

Rory and I took a deep breath and cut together a showreel that we desperately hoped would "peel the faces" off the "jaded, seen-it-all-before" advertising agencies. Much to our relief it did and so we won our first commercial.

One commercial led to the next and very soon we were being viewed as the "up and coming," "the brat pack," the "newcomers to watch." Before our eventual demise, some even labeled us potentially the production house of the nineties. Budgets ran from one hundred thousand to three hundred thousand rands ($10,000 to $30,000) per commercial.

As executive producers, Rory and I were responsible for all aspects of production from all budgeting and financial aspects of television production through to the co-ordination of all producers, film directors, production managers, crew, cast, props, locations, studios, camera and lighting equipment hire, vehicle hire, film processing, editing, music and post-production.

The business leased a large house in the exclusive Johannesburg suburb of Sandton, with a swimming pool and tennis court, set in large grounds where our two South African Ridgeback dogs roamed. (We were upwardly mobile, remember ... the upwardly mobile in South Africa owned Ridgebacks!) They were simply gorgeous dogs that were treated like our babies. (Nik was also vehemently anti-yuppie but had a strange affection for us, which surpassed even his brand of intellectualizing.)

Well, the saga progresses. Our personal house was an unusual six-bedroom, three-bathroom thatched house in Bryanston and to complete the total picture, we were driving a brand new BMW cabriolet and a gleaming old black Daimler.

Over the months we started to build up credibility including the production of several high-budget, high profile commercials for a model agency, a well-known brand of designer sunglasses and the launch of a British newspaper into South Africa. We even landed the new "South African Police" commercial for a new South Africa.

Meanwhile all types were parading through the production offices, some of them rather strange characters. This included one extremely talented young film lighting cameraman (the flavor of the month in the industry) who used to arrive in his huge old black Mercedes, reminiscent of a hearse. Completely strung out on cocaine, he would pour out his addictive woes and, on occasion, challenge us to get him converted.

Towards the end of 1990, wild rumors started to circulate that the lady heading up one of the crew agencies was a witch and had put a curse on us because we were Christians.

And almost to convince us, disaster struck.

The South African political situation had created a highly volatile business climate and suddenly the big businesses started to cut back dramatically on their advertising budgets. The first thing to go in their advertising briefs were ... guess what? Yes: television commercials.

Clients were happy to keep what in the industry is labeled the "below the line," but the costly "above the line" sphere of high-budget television commercials was the first to disappear.

And the production houses that would suffer most were the new, young, brave houses that had minimal capital resources to ride the storm.

Now, we had also just finished shooting a music video for Mango Groove (one of South Africa's top music groups at the time) with Nik. And then it happened ... The "big boys" (the most heavyweight production house in Johannesburg) offered Nik a deal that he couldn't and *didn't* refuse.

And so he exited ... with some of our clients in tow.

45

Suddenly we were left sans the one commodity that we had invested all our time and energy in – *Nik*.

Enter two more middle-of-the-road, experienced film directors ... and their expense accounts, their long lunches ... producers ... production managers ... the list went on.

There was just one slight problem. Our overheads had doubled, but our film directors were spending more time "doing lunch" with our clients than actually bringing the work in or tying any adverts down.

We started off in 1991 pitching on over two million rands ($200,000) worth of advertising commercials. Normally we would win at least forty percent of this. We were awarded the "Pick and Pay" commercial from one of South Africa's leading supermarket chains, worth over a quarter of a million rands. A week later, because of the political climate, they postponed until the following year.

We were devastated. That commercial would have taken us through the rocky months to March.

Finally, we were awarded one more commercial worth one hundred and fifty thousand rands ($15,000). But at that stage, we were already trimming overheads frantically and had given some of our key staff notice. This included the film director nominated by the agency to shoot this commercial. To cut a long story short, he and his producer walked off with the advert.

Weary and exhausted from extinguishing minor and major fires, we decided not to go through the legal wrangle and concentrated our energies on pitching for a new airline account, which was also postponed.

By this time, if we were honest, we would admit that our aim had now become a desire to get to the top and to make as much money as possible while getting there, rather than to honor God in the industry. Pride comes before destruction ... and so the seeds had been sown.

Things went from bad to worse. Our Daimler was stolen. Our bank manager, who had been our most enthusiastic backer (we had given him Richard Branson's biography to encourage him!), finally started to pull the rug.

Whereas before, anything that we touched had turned to gold, now it seemed that there was only destruction all around us.

No matter where we tried to dam up the holes, or how we tried to rescue the sinking ship, nothing worked. There was a supernatural slamming of the door on any more of our upwardly mobile ventures and no matter how much we sought God or practically addressed the situation, there was no doubt about it – Alec-Gene was dead.

Because of our unwillingness to arrive in England with no security and by faith, we had been, in the permissive will of God, building up a house that was our own and not in the plan of God. We had been laboring in vain.

Even so, in the midst of the seeming defeat, favor was still round about us. We could have had a "bankruptcy" party and our clients would have come! Our creditors gave us grace beyond measure. It was almost as though everyone agreed that undoubtedly destiny was hovering over us, but it was to be in a different sphere.

To make it worse, by this time, I was six months pregnant. We lost our exclusive office furniture worth thousands of rands. We lost our beautiful house, our BMW (the Daimler was already stolen), the computers, fax machines, photocopiers, company vans and cars. Eventually circumstances were so pitiful that I ended up selling my clothes to be able to pay our faithful cleaner, Josie. Oh – how the mighty had fallen!

We arrived in desperation at Rory's parents' house in Rustenburg with our Ridgebacks in tow. Rory was still just twenty-five. We didn't even have money for an air-ticket to the UK.

We had lost *everything*.

Rory was by this stage so numbed that he would sit in front of the computer for hours at a time. I was seven-and-a-half months pregnant with no knowledge of what the next month held, let alone tomorrow.

The dream was shattered.

The twenty-fifth of August came and with it, a gorgeous nine-pound baby girl, Samantha Jean. She was a face presentation and after an almost full labor, I had to have an emergency caesarean. After the operation, I was desperately ill with an infection.

Rory and I were completely shell-shocked. What was *happening* to us?

We sensed that we had great things to achieve for God. We knew we were called – there was a specific destiny on our lives – but chaos was all around us. Where was God's plan? All we had ever wanted to do was to serve Him and work for Him. No matter how involved we had been in secular media, we had always wanted His will – but now what?

There was seemingly no sense, no comfort, and no direction. And so, we cried out to the Lord: "Make a way where there seems to be no way." And somewhere deep in our hearts in the midst of the horror and the pressure of closed doors, there was this spark that whispered "and now into the will of God."

CHAPTER FOUR

THE WASTELAND,
OR HOW THE MIGHTY
HAVE FALLEN

A ND SO – DEAR READERS – that is how the great and mighty, now the greatly fallen, happened to land in England in the late September of 1991. We stood on my parents' doorstep in Dorset (minus the Ridgebacks) looking like ex-inmates of a prisoner of war camp in our pallor, clutching our three-week-old baby and the princely fortune of eight hundred pounds ($1,400) (from Rory's grandfather) with a desperate air.

Much to my parents' relief (my father had offered the garden shed as a alternative place of residence if the baby continued to wake everyone five times a night), we managed to find a tiny two-bedroom flat in Thames Ditton, Surrey. Unfortunately the owners were not prepared to let us use the second bedroom, so we all slept together, which also meant that we all woke together whenever our baby Samantha woke – oh hallelujah!

In the midst of this there was great activity to try and keep Rory in England. (I had a British passport, Rory didn't.) After much fervent intensive prayer in front of the counters at the Home Office, at which I'm sure people thought we were muttering in Afrikaans, Rory was given the official stamp to stay in the United Kingdom indefinitely.

Then there was the next obstacle – how to survive.

While we had been producing commercials, a desire to see the Gospel preached through A-grade Hollywood films had grown in our hearts. We felt God had given us three major projects including a project called *The Antichrist* (which has developed into today's project – *The Chronicles of Brothers*).

At this stage we were not in any way interested in implementing Christian television. We considered it to be primarily fairly insular by nature and our burning desire was to *reach* the lost.

Unfortunately, a short time after our arrival in the UK, it became apparent that the film industry in the UK was not only struggling but fighting for its very survival. Anyhow, I managed to get myself a London film agent, and we linked up with a London design studio for the animated project and started to write a serious screenplay.

During this time, Rory met a fellow Christian brother at the church we had joined and they decided (which I will always believe was God's permissive will) to collaborate on some sports promotions in the now re-opening New South Africa as a means of raising some serious money.

After they had made an initial trip back to South Africa, the sports plans took a turn towards music promotions and they started to research the possibilities of taking music groups out to a country that had been starved of any international interaction for years.

So, while Rory and his colleague were plotting and planning their tours to South Africa, I was involved in the first few rewrites of a hundred and twenty pages of screenplay amidst nappies, bottles and decorating the flat lemon and blue (to get some relief from the mottled brown and purple carpet).

Also in this period, we attended two courses on professional Hollywood screenplay writing in London overseen by Ron Suppa, a tutor at UCLA (the University of Los Angeles) and producer of Sylvester Stallone's movie *Paradise Alley*.

We took the liberty of inviting Ron for lunch. He turned to us and said, "I *never* do this ... but I will." And so, over the months, a friendship grew.

The next step was Rory, myself and Samantha taking off for South Africa. Rory was taking Shakatak, the jazz-fusion music group, on a South African tour spanning the five-thousand-seater arenas in Johannesburg, Durban and Cape Town. Rory (the producer) was to set it up and his partner (the accountant) was to monitor it from London until two weeks before. Let me just say here – if you ever wanted a definition of gambling, it is *music tours!*

In addition Rory was about to experience an unparalleled crisis of faith. He had been born again at sixteen, but had up till this time lived quite a superficial Christian life. Often it had seemed that there was a barrier to his spiritual growth, which had always been beyond my understanding.

Because I had always needed God so desperately, I had been consumed with Him since that night of recommitment many years before, but Rory had always seemed to skim the surface with God. There were many times that I cried out in desperation for God to change Rory into His man but there was little visible transformation.

And so, there was Rory, fighting with God, fighting with himself and being lured into the glitzy world of secular promoting.

Well, I was praying so long and so hard ... The one thing that I was totally convinced of, was that my heavenly Father was not going to leave *any* stone unturned until this situation was brought to account.

Things became so pressurized that I almost returned to England, but God told me to stay and be strong. The tours started, and the press across South Africa raved about the concerts.

There was only one thing that would or could get Rory's attention in this present state and I knew exactly what that was ... and so did God ... it was *money*.

Rory's business partner came out and was shocked at the way Rory was behaving and at his hardness of heart. His behavior spiraled progressively downward and then, as the last show ended in the prestigious Ellis Park stadium, amidst glowing reports and packed arenas, it appeared there had been a strategic mistake in setting up the tour – they were several performances too short.

If there were no extra concerts, they would lose a vast amount of money ... and it was too *late* to change it.

God finally burst the balloon. The tour lost approximately seventy thousand pounds ($125,000). God now had the hook He needed to start to pull Rory back in. This was because it was Rory personally who had raised the initial capital from the Christian investors and felt honor-bound not to let them down.

And so, he returned to England, still fighting with God, but with his back against the wall. In fact, I would say that God slammed his nose full-face *into* the wall!

You see, no one is exempt from deception, dear friend. Deception is deception because it is deceiving, and up to that time, Rory had been a spiritual baby. But then he turned full-face around and repented – a genuine, deep repentance and a true surrender. And probably for the very first time, God started to have proper access to his life.

Unfortunately, the pastor of the church we were attending took the attitude "Get in the Word." There was very little pastoring or getting alongside Rory. No personal ministry. He inferred that Rory should sit on the back row for at least six months and that they would watch his "fruit." In layman's terms, he was putting Rory *"on ice."*

Oh, but the ways of God are not the ways of man. How far superior are the purposes and plans of our heavenly Father. Where a man will look at the exterior, we have a God who sees through to the intents and purposes of the heart. How grateful Rory and I are for that.

Almost immediately the pastors of Cornerstone Christian Center in Bromley, Kent, approached Rory and me to assist them in setting up their ministry television department.

We tried every way that we knew how to convince them that they didn't need us, but they wouldn't take no for an answer. So the next and most vital step came into place and we joined the staff at Cornerstone Christian Center in Bromley, Kent.

I had already sensed that Rory needed deliverance from generational curses, especially that of Freemasonry. I had known, but had taken lightly, the fact that both his father figures were active Freemasons as their fathers had been before them.

But God was about to reveal, through a precious and discerning couple, that Freemasonry had a legal and watertight stranglehold over Rory's heart and mind because of unbroken generational curses.

Whilst the tours were going on, God had revealed to me that Rory was spiritually deaf, blind and hard of heart and that there had been a blockage to his spiritual growth for years. What we later discovered was that the actual vows made during the indoctrination of Freemasonry involved placing a black bag over the head (spiritually blind and deaf) and putting a knife to the heart.

This same couple prayed for Rory and he was set free in a manner that was truly remarkable. But this was only the beginning of his Damascus experience.

Now the only problem seemed to be that we were now placed on a meager ministry salary, which barely covered our mortgage. We found ourselves going backwards financially without making any inroads on the Shakatak debt.

It was during this time on the staff at Cornerstone that Rory, as any good producer would do, started to look for an outlet for the Christian programs that we were making at the church. On this basis, he started to meet and connect with many of the people in England who were then involved in trying to launch Christian television.

First, it was a total shock to realize that there was literally no daily Christian television in Europe. Second, everyone we met said that it was an *impossible* task. Then, we heard that even those with all the money and the power had also been unable to launch.

Well, that was all well and good; we were just looking for an outlet for the church programs. We still viewed Christian television with some suspicion as being ghettoized and not reaching out to a dying and lost world.

But during this period, Rory woke up with a strong conviction: "Launch Christian television into Europe."

We both looked at each other. There were literally *dozens* of people everywhere trying desperately to launch Christian television. Some of them had been trying for years! Why should we succeed where so very many others had failed? We daren't just move ahead on a good idea. We had to be sure that this was God.

But the conviction continued to grow until after several weeks of prayer and time spent before the Lord, we were convinced.

Rory had already investigated the possibility of putting the church program on the local cable company Nynex, and began to meet with some of the cable operators. During one secular meeting with several channel representatives, he met Lawrence Nugent, then Managing Director of the Black Identity Channel, known as BET International – now closed down.

Rory and Lawrence struck up an immediate affinity and a relationship started to develop. Rory started to explore the possibility of placing Christian programing on BET each Sunday morning. Finally, after Rory's persistent persuasion the first Christian programing ever shown on cable in London was placed on BET.

Where God anoints, He opens the way. Rory and I have an apostolic prophetic call to the media on our lives. And part of an apostolic call is a bulldozing, a spearheading, a breaking through of new ground. God will confirm His word and His callings with signs and wonders, so Rory and I *expect* signs and wonders in the media.

And we sensed that God indeed would use this anointing to open up the secular television channel, BET International, to the Gospel. And that is *exactly* what God did.

The second minister that Rory placed on BETI was Dr Fred Price of Crenshaw Christian Center, Los Angeles. Then came Dr Creflo Dollar and others in quick succession, and a whole block of three-hourly ministries to be on once a week on the Black Identity Channel.

It was during this same period, however, that we met with Dr Morris Cerullo.

We were summoned in great anticipation to the Grosvenor House Hotel, in Mayfair, where we proceeded to share the vision that God had given us for the first Christian television channel in Europe with the man himself.

Dr Cerullo viewed us politely and with curiosity. He listened to these two young people and their envisioned presentation very patiently. Then he laid down his conditions. If any agreement was ever to be made, it would mean that he would own the Channel but that we would have the security of salaries and every assistance ever needed. He also suggested to Rory that he fly out and meet with David Cerullo, his son.

We explained that we were not looking at this primarily as a commercial venture, but rather as a ministry with a commercial foundation, for God had specifically spoken to us and said that no one ministry or investor could control the Channel. We would need to have creative and spiritual control over the decisions of the Channel or the vision could possibly be distorted.

Dr Cerullo smiled slowly (and I must add, with great compassion) and said, "In that case, you'll have to tough it out."

Rory nodded. He had been given a direct mandate from the Lord never to sell our birthright no matter how much material security or prestige was offered to us.

But the *hysterical coward* named Wendy seated next to him, on the other hand, having just discovered that she was pregnant with our second baby and with the mortgage payment looming near, was tempted to clutch Dr Cerullo's hand in desperation and say, "Yes, yes, I'll sign it ... Give me the papers ... NOW!"

By this stage, I would quite heartily have signed our life away for a "bowl of soup" and the sooner the better. We needed security. We needed infrastructure. We needed *capital!*

But of course, all I did, apart from a moment when my teeth almost bit through my top lip, was to smile sweetly (if with extreme pallor, which I'm sure was excused as morning sickness!), as Rory earnestly said ... "In that case, Dr Cerullo," there was a brief hesitation, "we'll tough it out, sir."

And needless to say, the heat started to blister through the desolate wasteland of launching Christian television wherein we wandered ... and with that brave sentence ringing in our ears, we left the sumptuous luxury of Mayfair and drove back in stunned silence to our much *much* humbler abode in East Molesey, Surrey.

CHAPTER FIVE

A NEW MAN

B̲y NOW, WE HAD MET a small group of Christian business-men who were excited about the vision. After much discussion and prayer, we all concluded that the best manner in which to achieve independence was to raise the money ourselves to finance Christian television.

Enter Ishmael ... in the form of GOLD.

First, from South Africa came an opportunity via Rory's father who was in the publishing business. One of the publications he represented was called *Mining Journal*. He had been approached by a small gold dealer in Ghana to export gold to Europe for which a seemly profit could be made. A very seemly profit.

Aha! Our eyes lit up (especially as so many Christian business-men in the UK that we had met at that time were by all accounts bankrupt or rapidly progressing that way) ... this must be God's provision ... *a gold deal!*

And so, the dastardly deal progressed.

Rory flew out to Ghana to see how the land lay. But God had a different plan in store for him. The morning after his arrival, he was woken at the crack of dawn by a young Ghanaian man by the name of Stephen.

Stephen was to arrange a meeting between Rory and Mr Philip Amoaku, a government official and the number two in the Geological Survey Department. Philip also happened to be Stephen's older brother.

Sitting on the veranda of this one-star hotel, Rory felt led to tell Stephen that the reason that he was in Ghana and interested in gold exports was because he was a born-again Christian and wanted to make healthy profits in order to fund Christian television in Europe.

Stephen's face lit up, exclaiming that he too was born again!

Rory and Stephen ended up having four hours of private church that morning. Rory sat, aghast at the wisdom of the Holy Spirit pouring from this young man, as he quoted scripture after scripture, hour after hour, without a Bible in sight.

Stephen met with Rory again the next morning, with the Holy Spirit once again moving profoundly through this young accountant. Then Stephen announced that his older brother, Philip, would meet Rory on Tuesday.

During this time the gold dealer was stalling on Rory, claiming that before negotiations could proceed, Rory would have to meet the Chief of this particular tribe who were trying to sell their gold output.

Rory arrived with Stephen at the government offices in Accra to meet Philip. Well, compared to the godly Philip, Stephen was but a spiritual *babe!*

"The Man of God said you would come," said Philip.

Rory looked at him questioningly.

"Two years ago, he told us a white man would come who would bring Christian television to Europe. He knows you are coming and now you are here."

Rory's eyes nearly fell out. "I will tell him you are here," continued Philip.

At this point, the gold deal started to pale into insignificance as God's greater plan and His sovereign purpose started to manifest themselves.

Rory dutifully met the persons involved in the exporting of the gold, looked over their operation and requested more detailed paperwork and their government credentials before Philip appeared.

"The Man of God will meet with you. God has said he must pray for you!"

Now by this time, it had become very evident to Rory that Prophet Kwame, as he was called, was no ordinary pastor.

In the next few days, whenever he had free time after finishing his business with the gold company, he would spend his leisure time with a growing group of the "Man of God's" disciples. They were all the same. They radiated the glory and the power of God.

Rory started to learn more about Prophet Kwame. He had been a sinner and one night, the Lord Jesus had appeared to him personally and his whole life had been transformed. There were stories of miracles and talk of "the fear of God descending," so much so that the night before Rory was to meet him, he became exceptionally uneasy.

Rory phoned me from Accra to say that he really felt that he should stay to meet with him and I just knew by the sound in his voice that something profound was taking place.

God was preparing to clean up any left-over residue from Rory's old life and a supernatural impartation was about to take place that would mean Rory Alec would never be the same man again.

Well, dear readers, I received my husband back a new man. Not a *changed* man ... but a *new* man. It was as though Rory had been born again for the first time. How can I describe it? There was something awesome about what had taken place in Rory's life and it was evident for all to see. He was transformed. A supernatural fire now burned in him for God.

And so, for the first time since I had been married to Rory, I stood in awe as I sensed a call of God on his life so strong that I knew this was the same kind of call that had operated over other apostolic men that God had raised up to fulfill His purposes.

There had been an impartation that had released the fullness of an apostolic anointing to shake the foundations of Satan's previously held media bastions. But more than that, there was now in evidence a call to the five-fold ministry, an anointing that would grow with the months as a fire to preach the Gospel, as God had intended for him since the beginning of time.

God never leads without equipping. It is often said that "Where God guides, He provides" and indeed God had by a powerful, sovereign impartation through the Holy Ghost started to equip Rory for his role in the mammoth apostolic work that would lie ahead.

I sense that there are many, many women reading this book who sometimes may despair that your husband could ever take hold of God. That for so many of you would be your greatest desire.

The truth is, dear friend, that for the first six years of our marriage I lived sometimes in an unspoken despair that my husband seemed to continually live on the outskirts of God but never seemed to be able to make that vital connection. I longed for a husband who would pray for me, and wash me with the water of the Word ... a husband who would be such a leader and priest of our home. And I cried many, many, *many* heartfelt tears behind closed doors, because it is an incredibly lonely walk when you walk alone with God in a marriage. Especially if your husband is already saved but not able to walk in the fullness of God's destiny for him.

I have learnt many things over the years that I wish so much that I had known then. If only we could see the future, it would give us so much hope. But it can be especially hard when it concerns our own loved ones.

So, I say this to any of you today who are struggling in the private place of your own home. Where your greatest desire is that your own husband (or wife) would be touched by God in a profound way so that you could walk together more fully in the spirit.

Even when we were first married, several friends of mine didn't feel that Rory had any significant call on his life. I often despaired, because I had such a fervent burning call to the prophetic and to media. But you see, often God actually has TIMES and SEASONS and I believe with all my heart that with some people He also has ignition keys.

So, today, if your husband or wife may seem lukewarm or backslidden, dear friend, please take heart in what we went through. I prayed and prayed so many years and saw no change. I was at times desperate – then gave up in frustration, followed by despair. But you see, our wonderful heavenly Father hears every cry. The man that you despair of today could truly, TRULY be the Billy Graham of tomorrow. If you can just hold on, no matter how small that mustard seed of faith may seem to you, God is such a mighty, mighty God and He can and WILL indeed work miracles on your behalf. I stand today, eleven years later at the side of a strong, growing young apostle who in years to come I have no doubt God will continue to raise up as one of His mighty, mighty men on the earth. If God could turn my despair – and our union into such a powerful pioneering union for the Gospel in this century – what can He not do for you???? He is still the God of the impossible.

Father, I lift each and every man or woman today who is reading this book right now and who has given up on his on her spouse in despair and desperation. And Father, I break the power of the stronghold that keeps their spouse ... in bondage in the mighty

61

name of Jesus Christ. I break the shackles from their arms and legs. I break the blinkers of blindedness from their eyes, from their minds in the mighty, mighty name of Jesus Christ. In that powerful Name, I loose their ears to HEAR the voice of God. I loose their eyes and spiritual eyes to SEE the works of God and the hand of God. We release them from the bondage of the enemy right NOW in the Name of the Lord Jesus Christ of Nazareth. And I cry "FREEDOM! FREEDOM! FREEDOM!" to their minds. To their hearts. Release them, Father, from areas of sin. Convict them, Father of all hidden, unconfessed sin. Liberate them from every bondage.

And now, dear child, the Lord would say – "This is a new day. This is a new season. Even now the hope that wells up in your heart is hope from Me. And as you place your hand in Mine. And as you rise and lift your face to Me, I tell you that a new day dawns upon you – And it is not the day of the things of the past. For the day of the past shackles are broken," says the Lord – "And the season of liberation for your marriage, for your family, for your home dawns upon you. So take heart, precious child. Take heart, lift your head. Dry your eyes. And trust in Me."

CHAPTER SIX

A PROPHET ON TIME

R ORY WAS NOW an associate minister of the church in Bromley. We were working very hard to develop the television department there and after a brief discussion, and with much wisdom on their part, the pastors acknowledged that God was indeed separating us out for the sake of the Gospel and the calling on our lives. (We would eventually resign from being staff members a few months later with their full blessing and encouragement.)

At the end of July, our church was involved in a prophetic convention and we attended the Friday meetings as part of the staff. We had never been the kind of people who would run after the prophets. We believed that God was well able to intervene prophetically if He chose to do so, and we were happy to leave prophetic confirmations in His hands.

But something different stirred in our hearts that Friday. We watched as Jonathan David, a prophet from Malaysia, started to move under the prophetic anointing.

Here was an anointing *so* accurate and *so* profound that

together, without knowing it, Rory and I both sensed that God would speak and confirm His call on our lives through His prophet. The meeting came and ended but there was no word for us.

It was my father's birthday on the Saturday, so we could not attend the next day's meetings. We walked away, slightly discouraged.

Unknowingly, we had *both* felt that God had something for us. But there was nothing to do but to walk hand-in-hand with God ourselves and continue to take the steps of faith required.

However, when we arrived at church, two Sundays later, who should be preaching in the morning service but Jonathan David. We were seated right in the comer, tucked away out of the camera's reach.

Jonathan David started to preach. Suddenly, about a quarter of the way into his sermon, teaching on the Apostolic Breakthrough Church, he hesitated briefly, saying, "There are people in this place who are going to raise up television networks as never before ... as never before."

He reverted back to his sermon, then stopped and asked for those involved in television: he said, "All those who have this 'passion' for television, stand up." Then, he turned straight to Rory and me tucked away in the corner and pointed his finger directly at us.

He looked at us with the fire of God gleaming in his eyes and started to prophesy. "God shows me that you are like a stone cut out from a different place. God brought you here that you might become part of what He is doing here, and right across Europe, right across Germany..." (At this stage, we were only looking at cable in England.) The complete prophecy is at the front of this book, but the most profound thing was that by the end of this prophetic word, Jonathan David was talking specifically about a television network that would turn the destiny of entire churches, a network that would change the destiny of the Church.

This prophecy was given on 31 July 1994 and now we watch this prophetic word come to pass every day, as GOD TV works alongside the local church, helping it to be effectively equipped for today's end-time harvest.

As I look back on our 2002 Battle for Britain evangelistic initiative, I see how the GOD Channel has started to impact the Church. During this time, more than two thousand churches throughout the UK partnered with GOD TV to win the lost, and every day we receive letters from pastors telling us how effective a tool the Channel is to help bring congregation members to maturity.

God used a prophet from Malaysia, who knew nothing about us, didn't know us from a bar of soap, to say, "Yes, My children, this is My work, this is MY mandate to you. Be strong and very courageous and run with what I have commanded you that Europe shall be saved."

And so we said, "Yes Sir!" And started to run.

As well as working for the church, placing ministries on BETI and starting to contact the British cable operators, we attended the "Believers' Convention" with Kenneth and Gloria Copeland in late August 1994.

Now, of course, we were invincible. We had the assurance that Father God Himself was behind us!

Anyway, back to August 1994!

We continued to contact the cable operators and they were intrigued at this new potential subscriber base, but cautious as to the controversy surrounding Christian programing, particularly as relating to the American televangelists. Basically one and all agreed that when we were up and running, they would, more often than not, carry us, but until then they could not forward us the letter of intent we so desperately needed to raise the funds necessary to launch.

So, at this stage, we return to the gold deal, which was still pending. Rory had met briefly with Dr John Avanzini, a teacher of biblical economics and he had advised that indeed to preserve independence we should try to raise our own money to launch.

The natural solution was, of course, we concluded – the gold deal.

Oh, hallelujah – would we never learn that God wanted all the glory out of launching Christian television in Europe, not to give it to a group of Christian businessmen or to a good deal that Rory made? But of course, the brick wall was looming up again.

By this time, we had resigned from Cornerstone Christian Center and I was eight months pregnant.

Calls to and from Ghana were now generated in a flurry. The refinery was set up in the UK to receive the gold. Then it would be sold on the open market in London.

Everybody was working intensively on this deal. Contractually, it would mean that for twelve months we would receive a shipment of unrefined gold at Heathrow and resell it onto the open market, making an excellent profit of which our share would be enough to run the then cable channel for a year. This we felt was a really comfortable arrangement.

Well, the lawyers and accountants had started to set things up. And Rory's father was even flying in from Johannesburg to spend a night with us in the UK before going on to Accra to do the final groundwork.

I should mention that during this time, on the second of December, I delivered our gorgeous sunny second baby, a little boy who we named Christian Alec. The consultant advised another caesarean as he warned that this was likely to be a large baby. Christian weighed in at ten pounds and four ounces.

Straight after the birth I hemorrhaged badly. After the nurse's initial panic, I was settled in the emergency room. My parents and Rory left. Well – there I was, still in the emergency room, *sans* make-up, looking as if I had been dragged in from the African bush, when suddenly in burst three excited men with "gold-fever" written all over their brows: Rory, his father and a colleague.

I was handed a few bunches of wilted hospital flowers, some strange sort of daisy which looked as if they had seen better days, and the conversation that night in the emergency room seemed to center more on the gold than the fact that we actually had a new son. (Well almost!)

And here comes Hollywood, guys. The Ghanaian gold dealer gave them a kilogram of gold dust as security. Nine thousand dollars was paid to allow the release of the container onto the plane, which never did take place! Five days later, the gold was tested and it disintegrated ... it *was* fake! Nearly nine months' work in ashes ... and of course, the dealer disappeared off the face of the planet ... with *our* dollars.

Well now there was a Proverbs 31 wife with our one-week-old baby boy, acting strangely like another wife in a certain more unflattering section of Proverbs! Both Rory and I had resigned from the church, our commission from Christian Media Placements would only be paid to us at the end of January ... do you know, dear readers, we had *twenty pounds ($35)* to last us over Christmas!

Now we had been through hard times before and when we first arrived in England there were times we didn't have groceries in our cupboard, and I couldn't buy Sam clothes, but this was about the worst one we'd experienced yet!

We slunk down to my parents with not even enough money to buy presents for the family, Rory looking slightly pale every time my mother asked him about the progression of the gold deal. When my brother, the newly budding doctor, and his wife came on Boxing Day, that was the final straw. Now we not only felt like the poor relations – we *were* the poor relations!

My father, who had me completely taped, would look at me

suspiciously and mutter, just within ear shot, remarks inferring that he thought "born-again Christians" were supposed to be radiant, not going about his house scowling darkly!

And so we made our way back up to Surrey, with nothing to come back to in the natural. The dream was completely dashed, the cupboards were bare, the baby that I had vowed would have every-thing seemed to have been born into a worse state than his sister. My stitches were still sore, but as I worshipped my Father God, there was a deep assurance that all would be well and in His hands. We took the most rational and sensible step and we went on income support (Social Security).

God, in His infinite wisdom, allowed us to go through many things.

Rory and I know what it's like to live the high life, but we also know what it's like for thousands out there who are on income support and have to get by on very little. We know what it's like to fail and to hardly have enough to clothe the children. Friends, I know what it is like not to be able to buy the baby new clothes. I know how it feels to be cooped up day after day with a tiny one, not knowing if life will ever change. Oh precious people – if our wonderful Father God can bring us through – He can bring *you* through too.

CHAPTER SEVEN

ASTRA

S0, THERE WE WERE, at the beginning of January 1995, with the prophetic word that God would launch a Christian television network, through us, but with all our dreams in tatters. Then, in the second week of the new year, Rory woke up and said, "God wants us to go for Astra."

"Astra!" I exclaimed, interpreted as, *"Have you finally gone completely insane ... How are we going to feed the BABY?"*

The Astra satellite system was the most highly sought-after satellite system in Europe at the time, beaming its signal into over twenty-two million homes across Europe (four and a half million of those in the UK), a potential sixty-five million people across twenty-four nations. Every significant television channel was on this satellite and we knew beyond any doubt that in the natural it was completely impossible to gain access to Astra. We had been regaled with stories of how the most powerful ministries and groups of Christians had tried to get access to the Astra system with absolutely no success.

And now, after months of negotiating with different cable

operators, and still not having a definite offer of carriage, the thought of going through months of trying to access this most prized satellite system was almost soul-destroying.

But I *knew* that God had spoken and we were in the position where either Rory would have to go and get a job in the secular media, or we would choose to pay the price required and follow God's call. Deep in my heart I knew that we COULD NOT give up now. That's what pioneering is about. But it would take every bit of courage we possessed to continue.

It was the first week of 1995; we had a three-year-old little girl and a four-week-old baby boy. We were faced with a dashed gold deal, cable operators who were sitting on the fence and not even a glimmer of light for our future. But deep inside both of us, there was still something that whispered, "Fight ... don't give up ... don't give up now."

Rory phoned Astra's headquarters. They were not the slightest bit interested to hear about Christian television. He spoke to our media legal consultants, who said it was impossible.

Ministries we were in contact with, said: "Impossible – we've tried, can't be done." *Every* place we turned to for wisdom and advice stated quite categorically that accessing the Astra satellite system was the ultimate impossibility.

But the requirement necessary to break through Satan's iron grip on the media, and specifically the Astra satellite, was the anointing to fulfill the task. And yes, many had gone before us, but this is where God's prophetic destiny for us as individuals was about to run its course.

God required new wine for a new wineskin. He was not going to allow old wine that had been used to spearhead Christian television into other parts of the world to simply transplant to Europe, because He had a brand new and unique agenda for Europe.

And deep in our hearts, we began to sense that the reason that there had been so many casualties in Europe was because what was required to open up the gates to Christian television in dark, stiff-necked Europe would be the Living God's apostolic anointing to the media.

The apostolic is a breakthrough, foundational anointing ... an anointing that would be able to confront the strongholds of darkness over the continent of Europe and boldly challenge the Prince of the Power of the airwaves.

But without that breakthrough anointing, we believe, many dear, well-meaning people were hurt and wounded in their heroic attempts to launch Christian television into Europe.

God had also equipped us with the gift of faith and with this gift comes a tremendous boldness to overcome opposition and impossibility. He also knew that we would not just produce a Channel that was to be a "bless me" club, for the apostolic encompasses all elements of the five-fold ministry. This Channel was to teach and preach, to evangelize, to pastor and to impact Europe prophetically. The Christian Channel/GOD Channel would herald a REVIVAL.

Another result of an apostolic call to the media is that it will affect the secular media. And that was the second requirement that God had for His launching of Christian television – that it was to be a sign and a wonder in the midst of an unbelieving generation. I have stated earlier that often Christian projects that Rory and I were involved tended to attract attention in the secular press, and so, God once again would confirm His call and His anointing for His mighty end-time purpose in Europe.

Later, when many were saying, "You came out of nowhere" and the ones who had been faithfully working at Christian television for years were calling us "young upstarts," we knew that it was no mistake or accident that Europe had remained closed for a specific time.

God's attention is riveted on Europe and the part it will play in these end-times. The coming revival in Europe is a revival that will sweep the nations of the earth. And God has a timetable, and His timetable cannot be pushed forward by man.

And so, a hundredfold thanks to all those who have faithfully prayed for Christian television, and what a great debt is owed to each one of God's faithful intercessors, for indeed it is the intercessors that clear the way for God's chosen warriors to fight the battle.

God's chosen, appointed vessels may not, to the natural eye, be the most established or the most learned ... but as young David went out to face Goliath in God's ordained battle plan, so I believe that we were sent out by the Living God to literally demolish the jeering Goliath in Europe despite his continual taunts of, "Where is your God amongst all this filth and adultery and pornography and violence? Where is this God that so many of you in the UK and Europe say you serve?"

Now, Christians across Europe can *boldly* rise up and shout: "Here is the sign and the wonder in the midst of a perverse and unbelieving generation – here is God's sign across Europe – that the iron curtain of the media in Satan's kingdom will never again be the same as it was before the first of October 1995."

We will devote a chapter to the cynical press later, now back to Astra.

Rory contacted the leaseholders on the Astra satellite. Three came back to us for discussion. And the biggest miracle of all was the fact that one of them was no less than BSkyB – jointly owned by Rupert Murdoch.

Sky were prepared to enter into preliminary negotiations with us and furnish us with a letter of intent on condition that we received our ITC license (a license to broadcast courtesy of the Independent Television Commission).

72

CHAPTER EIGHT

THE AMERICAN DREAM

WELL, NOW WE HAD to win over the Independent Television Commission.

It had taken another Christian organization up to eighteen months to obtain their ITC license, and by all accounts, in the natural, we could once again be on the verge of a very long haul.

Apart from that, we needed credibility. We needed lawyers and accountants and large bank accounts and religious organizations. So we looked around to marshal anyone and everyone around us who seemed to fit the category. By the end of our paperwork, our company secretary was a Jewish firm of Trustees who handled millions of pounds' worth of pension funds each month in an offshore account. Our lawyers were the prestigious Simpkins (one of the most reputable set of media lawyers in London), among other strategically placed and credible names.

Then came a call from the ITC, brushing all of the pomp and ceremony aside and saying, "No, no – we want to know about Rory and Wendy Alec."

Well, our hearts in the natural were in our boots; this was like literally taking little David and bringing him before Saul to study his credentials. Other soldiers would have had a list as long as their arm of strategic battles, winning medals for service and for valor, and on David's application there would just have been "Fought a lion. Fought a bear."

And so we filled in our "lion and bear" application and waited with bated breath.

It was now the beginning of March. We had also, at the same time, remortgaged our house to payoff some of the lawyers' and accountants' bills and to enable us to survive.

Rory was booked to travel to Amsterdam to share the vision with a group of Christians working in the media in Europe, set up by Bert Panhuis who organized the occasion while I held the fort.

On the Wednesday that he was to speak in Amsterdam, our ITC license application was taken to board level (because it was a religious license) and the decision as to whether or not Rory and Wendy Alec could launch a religious channel across the United Kingdom and Europe was to be taken. (Strongly imprinted on our minds was the length of time it had taken the other religious license holders to get approval.) Rory arrived and was confronted by approximately fifty curious and some unsmiling, severe faces.

There were those who were excited about the vision, but then again there were those who had themselves been involved in Christian media for years and viewed Rory and me not only as young upstarts, but as downright arrogant – to think that "we" could dare succeed where so many older, more experienced people, who had been faithful for years, had failed.

Everything hinged on the decision that afternoon. If we didn't get our ITC License, we had no Christian Channel and no deal with BSkyB.

74

So there was Rory in Amsterdam and me down in the New Forest in Dorset, with my parents and the children, and our whole destiny hinged in the natural on the ITC board's decision.

Rory arrived back home, after his sharing of the vision followed by interrogation by some of the skeptics in Europe, feeling rather flat. He started to thumb through the pile of post waiting for him at home (mostly bills). Well, there at the bottom of the pile was a largish envelope that was stamped by the ITC.

Rory picked it up. Later he admitted that he started to brace himself for the long haul that everyone was expecting to be the next step, with all kinds of appeals for information pertaining to us and the Channel – the beginning of a logistical nightmare.

Well, dear friends, our God is *a wonder-working, miracle-working God*, for there in the envelope was a letter that stated "We are pleased to award the Christian Channel Europe a license from the Independent Broadcasting Commission to broadcast for ten years."

Our secular media lawyers, who dealt with these applications as a matter of course, said that they had never seen an application processed so quickly. They said that they must have literally got up from the board meeting on the Thursday and processed the license to arrive in the post by Saturday morning. Where God guides, He indeed provides!

Needless to say there was much rejoicing in the New Forest on Rory's arrival and now, it was time to take a trip to the "land of milk and honey" … America – here we come!

By this time all our funds were depleted with lawyers' and accountants' fees, with telephone bills to the States and living expenses, but there was still an inner sensing that we *must* take this trip.

A week before we were supposed to leave, we were at a church in Brussels and a prophetic word was spoken over us by a visiting

American speaker that we would be traveling within ten days and would receive great favor with men. Well, immediately we put two and two together. "Great favor" equals money.

To cut a long story short, the day before we left, no funds had come through. Then a certain pastor, with a church in Europe, said he knew we *had* to go and therefore he was prepared to cover the credit card expenses (of a fourth party traveling with us) in the unlikely event that we raised no money.

You see, this was now subtly turning into the "money" trip. We were totally convinced that as soon as America heard our vision to launch the first daily Christian television network in Europe, and knew that we had a firm offer from BSkyB and an ITC license, that the thousands of dollars would come pouring in. In fact the hundreds of thousands!

So, we left, in great faith, with total assurance that this was the trip to raise the funds necessary to launch the Christian Channel. Welcome America – first stop Chicago, to meet with Jerry Rose, founder of WCFC Chicago.

Well, we sat with Jerry and his right-hand man, Dave and enthusiastically shared the vision. What we didn't know at that stage was that America had been literally wrung dry with well-meaning people attempting to raise funds and support for their dreams of Christian television in Europe. And of course, none of these ventures had ever seen the light of day.

Now, let me say here that Jerry and Dave were extremely personable and I think that Jerry himself identified with us, thinking back to his own initial years of struggle, but we left the next day with basically a pat on the back and a smile.

The next stop was off to Marion, Illinois to meet with Garth Kuns and his wife; then after a flurry of phone calls made at an American motel, we finally managed to get an appointment to meet with Paul Crouch (founder of Trinity Broadcasting Network) in Nashville.

We were taken to the dressing rooms after the live presentation of "Praise the Lord" where we met for about twenty minutes with Paul Crouch.

He again was extremely courteous and asked for a proposal, but we sensed that he too had met so many previous Christian TV in Europe enthusiasts that he probably looked at the vision of this young couple and placed it on the shelf to see if it would come to pass.

We were learning fast.

It seemed that in America until your vision was established, there would be a reluctance to assist in any concrete way. We had come over believing that *this* was the nation that operated by faith, *these* were the visionaries, only to discover that there seemed to be a tremendous reserve towards any vision that wasn't already tangible.

This was becoming hard for all of us to understand. God was *vitally* interested in Europe, but Europe didn't have a vision or understanding of Christian Television. Was *no one* going to see the tremendous mission-field that could be reached through Christian television? Was everyone *only* interested in the commercial aspect of what they got out of it? Did no one think about *souls* any more? Had they all *forgotten* that they too had started by faith? Would *everyone* insist on controlling the vision?

What we later learned was that many, many well-meaning people, among them several opportunists, had approached these people that *we* were now approaching. In fact they had been approached to get behind Christian television in every obscure part of the world, and hardly any of these visions had actually come to fruition. So of course, when we came along all fuelled up with vision and passion, they had seen it all before.

"But we are *different!*" we exclaimed.

And they would all smile patiently and nod, saying, "Keep us updated on your progress. God bless you." And with a shake of the hand, they would be gone.

Each meeting became more disillusioning, and slowly we were becoming discouraged.

It became evident that no one in America was going to support us until we actually launched; that the *only* thing that would convince America of our credibility was not, as we had hoped, the firm offer from Sky and our ITC license, but the actual *existence* of the Channel.

Oh, where were the men and woman of faith and vision, who would be prepared to step out on the water with us? But you see, dear reader, God was putting us through *His* school.

However, I have to tell you, the fire of God in Rory and me could not be extinguished. They could ignore us, they could tell us we would end up like other casualties of Christian television, but *no one* would be able to extinguish the flame of the Christian Channel Europe, simply because *this* vision *was* birthed of God Himself.

But there were still no funds raised. Not one American cent.

We arrived at a church in Dallas just as an incredibly smooth, well-to-do gentleman climbed out of his gleaming new Jaguar. Not a hair was out of place, his trousers perfectly creased . . . here in front of us was this charismatic legend in person, staring at us, I might add, with a vague curiosity.

He showed us round his new television studio and then proceeded to take us into a private room. He looked at us with an even vaguer curiosity, which continued all through our presentation of the vision, (which was remarkably less impassioned, now that we had been battered by the winds of American ministry skepticism).

The above-mentioned gentleman saw immediately that the desperate, overriding need was, of course, financial. And here, I must say, all credit to him, he immediately said, "Let's pray and see what God says." And here it started. Immediately, he started to groan. And dear reader, I mean ... GR ... OA ... OA ... N.

Our eyes were on stalks, all staring at him together, until we remembered our manners and closed them rapidly. He continued to groan remarkably loudly. But this time we were each just opening *one* eye, at intervals, staring like John Cleese.

"You've got to GROAN ... REALLY GR ... OA ... OA ... N," he commanded us.

And so, we *all* started to groan in a more suitable manner.

After several minutes (it seemed more like an hour), he furrowed his brows. His eyes were closed tightly.

"I sense God has given me a figure ... He's saying ... "

We all leaned forward in anticipation.

"The figure is ... " Another long, drawn-out groan.

Our leaning now was stretched to the limit as we waited with bated breath (this had in the past been an extremely cash rich ministry until the scandal which shook it to its foundations).

Now, all of us, great propagators of "God is our source," suddenly looked disgustingly interested in this figure.

"I've almost got it ... " We stared goggle-eyed, looking remarkably like the leaning tower of Pisa, just waiting for the looming figure.

"I've *got* it!" We all opened our eyes as he looked up suddenly in triumph.

"It's five thousand!"

We all nearly fell backwards.

Oh Father, forgive my sense of the ridiculous, but the thought that immediately flashed through my mind was that with all that remarkable groaning, the figure would have been at least fifty thousand. (But unfortunately when the rubber hit the road, this gentleman reneged on the five thousand dollars.)

And so there we were, standing at the airport about to fly home, discouraged and disillusioned with nothing to show from our grand trip to America but a debt of ten thousand pounds ($18,000).

Oh *where* was the great favor that we had been convinced we would find with these men? And where was the funding?

But you see, dear reader, our wonderful heavenly Father had allowed us to realize at an early stage of the vision, that for all our lip service as to God being our source, it was very evident that we had subtly started to shift our eyes onto men.

We arrived back from the land of milk and honey tired and, I have to admit, almost shell-shocked. We had gone out in such high hope, with such expectation that God would achieve His miracle to launch the Christian Channel, and to all intents and purposes, it was a trip that had not only seemingly failed in its purpose but we had now discovered, as do all of God's pioneering eagles . . . we were flying alone.

It was a valuable lesson that we would never forget.

CHAPTER NINE

B S KY B

WE WERE NOW in an interesting situation. We had put off signing with BSkyB, believing that the money we needed as a deposit would have been raised in America. However, this had not come to fruition.

Now, we were faced with a dilemma. *Should* we sign the contract without a brass farthing in the ministry bank account or *should* we wait until the money was forth-coming?

Our secular media lawyers advised us in strong terms that to sign with no money could be seen as fraudulent. But there was a strong feeling inside our spirits that kept urging us, "Sign, Sign." We were waiting every day for BSkyB to carry out a credit check on us and to demand at least a fifty thousand deposit when we signed.

But the days passed and there was no credit check and no request for a deposit. Even our media lawyers shook their heads in wonder and amazement.

Well, the date was set to sign with the General Manager of BSkyB on 14 June 1995.

You cannot imagine the magnitude of that event to the Christian Channel. Our enemies, the skeptics, were indeed lined up against us. "They will never launch," was the devil's taunt.

But we determined not to be discouraged and set our faces like flint. You see, in the Word of God there had been a taunting just as intimidating when David faced Goliath.

"The Philistine also said to David, 'Come to me, and I will give your flesh to the birds of the sky and the beasts of the field!'"

(1 Samuel 17:44 NASB)

And the devil taunted *us* saying, "Everything's going to come crashing down around you, no airtime, no reputation, no television channel – everything will be destroyed. And you will be the laughing stock of all the skeptics and the cut-throat secular British media."

"Then David said to the Philistine, 'You come to me with a sword, a spear, and a javelin, but I come to you in the name of the LORD of hosts, the God of the armies of Israel, whom you have taunted. This day the LORD will deliver you up into my hands, and I will strike you down and remove your head from you. And I will give the dead bodies of the army of the Philistines this day to the birds of the sky and the wild beasts of the earth, that all the earth may know that there is a God in Israel, and that all this assembly may know that the LORD does not deliver by sword or by spear; for the battle is the LORD's and He will give you into our hands.'"

(1 Samuel 17:45–47 NASB)

And so, we turned to the Goliath of the media in Europe and we said, "This day the Lord will deliver Sky into our hand. We have been called to this from the beginning of time. This is not just a whim.

This is not our idea, but it is the mandate for Rory and Wendy Alec from the Living God that the Christian Channel shall be placed as a sign in the midst of a perverse and unbelieving generation, that Europe may know that there is a God in Israel, that there is a God in Europe.

"Then all the skeptics in Europe and America shall know that the Lord does not save with sword and spear (with money and power) but the battle is the Lord's and He will give the media into our hands."

With the sound of battle ringing in our ears, we decided that the time had come to sign with BSkyB.

And so, the following week, we made our way over to Osterley. You cannot imagine, dear reader, the exhilaration, the absolute awesomeness of finally walking into Sky to "possess the land."

Chris Mackenzie, BSkyB's general manager, was standing looking at us with a slight frown. He then turned to his legal advisor.

"Is everything in order, then?" he asked.

A deathly hush descended on Rory and me and the small group of faithful supporters who had accompanied us. At this point our legal advisors, who could not be there in person, were on the other phone.

We waited with baited breath, the great "faith people" trembling in their boots in case Chris Mackenzie decided at the last moment to ask for a deposit of fifty thousand pounds or *we were suddenly asked* to produce the dreaded credit reference. Chris Mackenzie frowned.

"Is everything in order?" The legal gentleman nodded studiously.

All eyes were now glued onto the piece of paper with the vacant signature.

Slowly, Mr Mackenzie picked up the pen and signed the document. He passed it over to Rory.

"I wish this was a check!" he quipped.

"So do I," said Rory, signing the papers enthusiastically.

Chris Mackenzie started and the ruddiness drained from his face, but he caught himself, turned, smiled, shook our hands and informed us that Rupert Murdoch was *not*, as many would believe, without any religious convictions, but was endowed with some finer Catholic sentiments.

This cheered us up. Maybe Rupert Murdoch would watch the Channel secretly in the early hours of morning and become an enthusiastic supporter. Ah! Of such stuff dreams are made.

But the deal was done. The contract was signed and we walked out praising and worshiping the living God.

We now had a watertight agreement with BSkyB. We had our license (a ten-year license) from the Independent Television Commission. We had been obedient to the prompting of the Holy Spirit and signed the contract. And within a short time period, we were to discover *why* we had felt the urgency to sign.

A few days later we received a telephone call from BSkyB informing us that now that we had a signed contract, they needed one of our hours back ... *urgently*.

Now originally, we had signed for the hours 7.00 am – 9.00 am. (CET) and Sky wanted the hour 8.00 a.m. – 9.00 a.m. back, but in its place, they would give us three hours from 5.00 a.m. to 8.00 a.m.

If we had not signed with them the week earlier, we would no doubt have received a phone call telling us that they needed the hour, but with no deal, in fact Goodbye to the first daily Christian television network in Europe.

But because we had been obedient to God's voice, they were *locked* into our contract. They couldn't budge without our agreement. They *had* to consider us. After much prayer we were convinced that although we would give up a premium hour, three hours would give us the space to broadcast "Kidz' TV", worship and Christian Music Television and allow us to present as a fully-fledged channel. Much better than just two hours of solid preaching. And here comes

God's miracle. In return for that premium hour, they gave us a one hundred and seventy five thousand pounds ($300,000) *discount* on our airtime for the year! Only God Himself could have worked out such a remarkable discount for us for giving up the hour that had suddenly become invaluable to Sky.

We discovered that Transponder 47 was fast becoming a premium channel. Now we were in the company of Sky Soap, Sky Sports 2, Sky Sports Gold, the History Channel and the Sci-Fi Channel. All these other channels were also only two to four hours a day, which made us the norm, rather than an outsider at an extended three hours.

But we had reached the stage where every penny we possessed had been utilized and all resources were depleted. We had our ITC license and a signed contract with BSkyB, but we had come down to the end of our arm of the flesh and now ... there was nothing left for us but God's miracle.

And so, on one sunny Friday morning in June, we arrived at the Heathrow Hilton where we were greeted by an enthusiastic young man called Trevor.

Well, we opened our hearts, exchanged the vision and left on our way to meet with a prophetic couple in Guildford.

They prophesied over us (which was taped), that God was going to give us access to equipment and a building and that in *but a few days* we would stand before two individuals who would have great significance for the Channel and ourselves. (Note: this was Friday afternoon.)

Still a bit battered from our April trip to America, we immediately placed the prophecy on the shelf.

Meanwhile, Rory was still believing for his air ticket back to America to meet with some other ministries and to reconnect with the men that we had met with on our previous disastrous American trip.

Truly, we were almost at the end of ourselves. We had walked by faith with God's dream in our hearts for so long believing that *surely* those we shared with would realize that this was indeed God's plan. God had worked His miracles and we now had an ITC license and a signed contract with Sky, but we were at our human limit.

All our personal resources were exhausted, our grocery cupboards were bare, we had a three-and-a-half-year-old little girl and a six-month-old baby (who was waking from four to six times a night). I was still suffering from violent nausea and weakness (I was convinced that some satanist had found out about the launch of the Channel and was sticking pins into an effigy of me!) and every possible avenue of funding was practically exhausted.

It was as though we were in the middle of a dark, black tunnel from which there was no escape no matter how we tried. After we'd been thrown into the pit, served time in Potiphar's house, we were now languishing in prison, forgotten.

The weekend came and went. Every envelope was pounced on avidly in case it was "the one," but five o'clock Monday afternoon (the deadline for Rory's air ticket) came and went, with no sign of a miraculous provision.

But you see, dear reader, our faithful, wonderful heavenly Father is the God of all compassion and mercies. He is the God of the impossible, the God who turned water into wine, the God who raised Lazarus from the dead ... and so, God was about to part our Red Sea in His ever miraculous way ... and our miracle started with a phone call at five-fifteen on this gloomy summer's day.

A phone call that was about to change the destiny of our ministry.

Trevor's voice rang loud and clear through the receiver.

"Benny Hinn wants to see you in London ... NOW!"

CHAPTER TEN

THE PARTING OF THE RED SEA, OR DESTINY ON A BUS IN LONDON

W ELL, THERE I WAS scrabbling for some semblance of make-up and the best remnants of our wardrobe (which I'm sure Joseph didn't do when he was summoned before Pharaoh!).

Our baby-sitter was available, miraculously at a moment's notice, and so we hit the A4 into London, praying that we wouldn't be held up too long by five o'clock traffic.

We arrived in London, found a parking space and literally ran over the street to where Trevor's big gleaming bus was parked outside the hotel in Chelsea. We were half-an-hour late. Yes, dear reader, we had kept Pastor Benny Hinn waiting in the bus for half-an-hour.

We climbed up the stairs of the bus, where we were greeted by Trevor, and turned to face the occupants.

Facing us was this arresting, elegantly dressed man who was staring at us intensely. In fact he looked at us quite sternly (we *were* late), and so we met Pastor Benny Hinn for the very first time.

We were then introduced to his associates and Pastor Benny's two elder daughters and the bus began its trip around London.

We started to share the vision of the Christian Channel Europe. Pastor Benny was, I must say, still staring at us with great scrutiny. I began to think twice about having chosen, in the flurry, my old faithful baggy black trousers.

Then, as we passed St Paul's Cathedral, Pastor Benny stopped the bus so that his daughters could see where they had filmed some of *Mary Poppins*. It was now pouring with rain.

Anyway, we all followed him out of the bus to look at St Paul's Cathedral and, rather drizzled on, we re-entered the bus and continued to share about the Channel.

By this time, I must add, the mascara I had used that day had reacted with my eye and was streaming all down one side of my face, and the rain had a disastrous effect on my hair!

So, there I was, feeling like a cross between the witch of Endor (from Shakespeare's *Macbeth*) and a London bag lady! facing these three men while Rory answered Pastor Benny's enquiries as to the Channel's reach and were we *really* going to be able to launch – all completely valid questions that we had answered many times before.

But suddenly I remembered that day in January, after our initial contact with BSkyB, when out of the blue the Father had spoken to me as clear as a bell and said, *"Benny Hinn* will help you."

Now, you must understand, that at that stage this was completely *impossible*. The truth is that all those years ago we actually didn't have a clue who Benny Hinn actually was. We literally had no idea of the magnitude of his ministry and the effect it was having worldwide. All I knew was that he was a man in a white suit who I had read had had an incredible encounter with the Holy Spirit.

We were also in contact on a much more personal footing with many other international ministries and their media buyers, who could and who, we were sure, *would* be the ones to assist us. We had tried to contact his office on a previous American trip – but to no avail.

But slowly and unmistakably, as Rory was reciting all the statistics back to Pastor Benny, the Father's voice came back as authoritatively as before: "I told you, Benny Hinn *will help you*." And I found myself flashing back to our time in America and the frustration we had encountered.

Was everyone *only* interested in the commercial aspect of what they got out of it ... did no one think *souls* any more? Had everyone who had had Christian television for years – had they all *forgotten* that they too had started by faith?

Was there *truly* someone who would see God's dream before it became a reality, who would see what God saw? Who would have the sensitivity and obedience to God to see beyond the two young people in front of them, beyond to a little David that could indeed overthrow the Goliath of the media in Europe? Did *everyone* want to control us?

And, finally, throwing all caution to the wind – it's easy to act as if you have no reputation when you quite patently *don't* have one! I am told that, with eyes flashing and (unfortunately) with my finger pointing (a bad trait!) straight at Pastor Benny, I blurted out, "Benny Hinn – have you forgotten how *you* started?"

There was a prolonged silence.

There I was, obviously staring at Pastor Benny in a rather fierce fashion with Kent, David and Trevor waiting with bated breath and Pastor Benny himself staring straight back at me.

And you know what, dear reader, suddenly the light of God broke through, and Pastor Benny's eyes started to twinkle with that simply marvelous Benny Hinn sense of humor.

Oh, our mighty, powerful God is never confused.

Pastor Benny not only shook hands on a commitment to put *This is Your Day* on the Channel twice a week, but he invited Rory over to America the next week to be a guest at his crusade in Louisville, Kentucky, to introduce him to several people that he felt could assist us in our launch.

We left London that day knowing that Benny Hinn indeed sensed that God Himself was involved with the Christian Channel Europe and was prepared to assist in any way he could.

We also left with Kent Mattox's air miles, with two hundred pounds ($350) as a love offering from Trevor (bless you Kent and Trevor!) and with the face of God shining on his two young servants as we drove back to Surrey radiant with new hope and the assurance that God had indeed started to part the Red Sea.

And sure enough, Rory arrived a week later in Louisville, Kentucky, to be at the crusade.

Well, Rory was looked after like royalty. Pastor Benny ensured that this young man from England had all his needs met. And then, God's counter-plan came into play, one evening of the crusade when Rory turned to be introduced to the couple next to him.

"Hello – I'm Rory Alec, from England."

"Hello – I'm Claude Bowers from Orlando, Florida."

After the crusade, Claude flew Rory back to Orlando to his own television station, Superchannel 55, where he shared the vision with Claude and his wife, Freeda.

God's plan was brewing.

On the Sunday morning, Rory went to Pastor Benny's church, the World Outreach Center, with Claude and Freeda. And so it was that during the meeting, Pastor Benny looked over, pointing to Rory and Claude, saying, "There's a divine connection between these two brothers." And indeed there was.

After the service Rory asked for Pastor Benny to pray over a handkerchief as a contact point for my faith (as an antidote to any satanic pin-sticking!).

However, I must confess that after a few weeks, the anointed handkerchief went through the wash (and the tumble dryer) and I always had these vague doubts as to whether the anointing had been tumble dried out ... (not quite the kind of question to ask at a partners' conference!). On top of that I seemed to have lost it in some obscure place, and became quite distressed for a few days, but I *was* healed!

Rory then flew back to London to rejoin us.

Almost immediately on his return, we received confirmation that Pastor Benny indeed *would* place his program onto the Channel twice a week and then, in the post, we received a gift of support from Benny Hinn Media Ministries – which was sent faithfully to us *every* month from the end of July right through to December. Only the Lord knows how much that gift meant to us. It sustained us through the very worst of times.

God weaves His will and His divine connections to implement His divine purposes ... and God in His infinite wisdom saw far beyond a little trip on a bus in London, through to a Christian television channel that would start touching millions of lives across the continent of Europe, and then move on to impact the nations. Interwoven in that plan was the crossing of Rory and Wendy Alec and Benny Hinn.

For you see, the world is about to witness a revival unprecedented, such as has never experienced before, a revival in which the GOD Channel as a transport system is gaining momentum each day every week, thrusting light forward into where previously only darkness has reigned in the midst of a stiff-necked and unbelieving generation, as a beacon of hope to the sick and the hopeless, showing forth God's love to a lost and dying world.

Truly, truly, I tell you, what we have thought to be the droplets of revival shall be as nothing in comparison to the mighty outpouring that is about to take place. And each ministry that is on the GOD Channel has been placed there by God Himself to turn the destiny of the churches across Europe, Asia, Africa, the Middle East and now America and bring salvation to those whose hearts are filled with despair and hopelessness.

Let us never forget the honor that is due to men like Benny Hinn and Claude Bowers and all those who had the compassion and conviction to assist this ministry in its fledging early months when all that could be seen in the natural was just a dream.

For truly, God never forgets ... and neither shall we.

CHAPTER ELEVEN

MONEY ... MONEY ... MONEY

W E WERE NEARING the end of June and Rory was back in London, but we were still no closer to launching. We had no investors and therefore no capital. By now, Paul Le Druillenec (who started his career as financial controller for Sky) had become the ministry's financial director. All of this activity was coming out of our lounge with one computer, one fax machine, one telephone line, the kitchen being our boardroom.

Most of our ministry clients had agreed to come on the Channel, the media buyers were all poised to sign the contracts and each day we were going forward towards the launch, but businesswise, we were totally stunted because of the lack of funds.

Every Christian businessman that we had been introduced to in Europe seemed to be suffering from the recession and had just lost his business or was about to go bankrupt. Every businessman that they were networked to was also suffering.

Even the Full Gospel Business Men's Fellowship International in Britain seemed to be having a wilderness experience. So many people were now enthused by the vision of the Christian Channel Europe, but nobody in Europe seemed to have a brass farthing to put together!!

We had been offered several deals, but each one of them involved the third party controlling the vision. This meant that they would be in control of all programing and would without doubt end up controlling the Channel. This would be directly opposed to what the Lord had specifically instructed Rory – that no other ministry or television network or group of businessmen could control the vision.

Rory had been clearly anointed in his role in GOD TV as the builder with God's wisdom and strategy when it comes to the deal making and business side of the ministry. I marvel at the tenacity and courage he continually shows as he protects the ministry and steers it forward. While I would have probably given away our birthright for a five pound note in our early days it's just as well that Rory continually said "NO!"

My role is creative/artistic director and Network controller – and then my tenacity kicks in with the issue of WHO and which programing appears on GOD TV. I HAVE to follow the Holy Spirit's voice because we have to follow His schedule in Heaven.

God had given us a direct mandate. First, the Christian Channel Europe was above all a *ministry*, before it was a business. Second, that God had a very defined programing schedule for Europe. His command to us was twofold – to broadcast the uncompromised Word of God and God's move of the Holy Spirit. The Channel was to be the Word and Spirit. God's promise to the fulfillment of this condition was that this Channel would spearhead *revival* through Europe and the world.

God had to be the Chairman of the board. We had to be free to put into operation everything that the Holy Spirit instructed us, or

God's plan for the Channel and its destiny in Europe and further afield would be watered down and could be aborted. This meant that only God's investor could fulfill all these conditions.

Now remember, Rory had met with Claude and Freeda Bowers in Florida. Claude had shown an interest in the Christian Channel, but we didn't know if it was a serious interest and if there would be strings attached that we could not accept. Claude was an anointed and shrewd businessman and we had now been around in Christian television long enough to realize that we needed to walk very circumspectly and with God's wisdom.

But the days passed and now our small team were working frantically to prepare everything for our launch date of 1 September. Still there was no capital. In fact, there was just *no money*, full stop.

Things had fast become more than desperate. Our telephone was cut because we could not pay the bill, Rory made his calls from the phone box with the Hampton Court traffic blaring out at sixty-five decibels. If the media buyers had known – they would have excommunicated us!

Two weeks into July we got so much to the end of ourselves that Rory finally decided to leave a message on Claude's answering machine about the possibility of his charity's involvement with the Christian Channel Europe ... just in case God had decided to use a man after all, and not just an angel to drop a wad of banknotes on the front doorstep! After some of the men we had met, we had more faith that God would use an angel and the wad of banknotes!

Well, Claude returned the call and booked his flight to come over to London, pointing out clearly that it was primarily to "shop."

On 21 July, we walked across Hampton Court Bridge from our house to the Mitre Hotel to meet with Claude Bowers. We sat across from him at the restaurant and poured our hearts out. He listened patiently and with great compassion as we unfolded the saga of the Christian Channel Europe in full technicolor. Oh! God bless you, Claude!

The following morning, we met in the boardroom of the hotel with our administrator and financial director to present the Channel's business proposal to Claude. We had come to the place where we knew beyond any shadow of a doubt that no man would be our source, but that God was *the only one* who could possibly give us the financial miracle desperately needed to launch the Channel into its next phase.

To all and sundry, we were an unknown quantity. God would have to speak supernaturally to someone's heart. This could not just be a cold-blooded, analytical business decision. On top of the investment, our other condition was that the investor could have *no say or control* in the running of the Channel.

The presentation finished several hours later. Claude was moving that afternoon to the Metropole Hotel in London and would then fly back to Orlando, Florida. On his return to America, he would present the information to *his* charity's board as to whether they would be prepared to give us the investment needed.

As we walked out of the room, Claude pressed something into our hands. It was a cheque for five thousand dollars.

God had seen our desperate and pressing needs, looked for a willing, obedient heart and had sent His servant all the way over from Florida to comfort us. This was but the beginning of our heavenly Father's goodness.

There we were left in London, standing (or rather staggering) in faith, on tenterhooks, sweating profusely at intervals, waiting for Claude's decision from America.

Oh, all of you out there who are right now in a desperate financial situation, who are believing for a financial miracle for your family or your ministry – take heart. Your God is the same miracle-working God who was about to pour out a financial miracle into our lives.

Less than a week later, Claude rang with a decision from the board. *(The incredible thing in destiny is that Steve Beik, our wonderful and dedicated Chief of Staff for GOD TV today was one of the five people on Claude's board who made that decision!)*

One hundred thousand dollars would be released as soon as the finer details could be worked out. Oh – how *good* God is when *His* purposes are involved. If He has to wake up a man or woman six thousand miles away to make sure that His project's needs are met – He *will* do it. He just looks for that obedient vessel who will listen and obey.

In fact, what was the greatest miracle of all was that, as we later found out, the board had actually made a decision to assist the Channel *before* Claude flew out to London.

But *we* didn't know that!

Once the finer details with the board were ironed out, the money would be released into an escrow account in London until we received the three approvals necessary before we could actually transmit our signal. But now we discovered that we needed a trust/ charity to receive the funds from America. Now what? This application to become a charitable trust was a process that could take up to two years!

Once again, God was about to provide in the most miraculous way.

We received a telephone call that same week from our secular media lawyers, who at that stage didn't know our need for a charity. They advised us that another set of clients, who had contacted them months earlier, had set up a charity to launch daily Christian television into Europe and were about to close everything down due to the lack of support.

Our administrator contacted Mr Maurice Raybould and discovered that a team of Christian civil servants and lawyers had spent 1991 to 1993 forming not only a charity, but a charity relating to *Christian television*. In fact, the notes and conditions of the charity deed specified *everything* that we as a ministry embraced.

Not only was this a startling discovery, but the trustees of this charity went before the Lord in prayer and agreed with one accord to hand over the charity, lock, stock and barrel to us.

God, in His infinite wisdom, had planned ahead and arranged for three experienced men with legal backgrounds to apply to the Charities Commission in 1991, with charitable status finally granted on 6 April 1993.

God had given us His *very own charity*, uniquely designed for the future GOD TV, the charity that our viewers know today as the Angel Foundation. Now it was time to negotiate for the second part of our launching capital! Rory and I appreciated Dr Morris Cerullo's willingness to upfront the year's fee as his contribution to the launching of God's miracle channel. It was Dr Cerullo's way of saying, "I believe God is with you. I'll support you." And so, this too went into our escrow account.

Now there was only one problem – *no* money could be released from the escrow account until we had the three approvals that Sky needed to be authorized before we could finally broadcast.

On 15 August, we had re-signed the contract with BSkyB for the new three-hour block from 5.00 a.m. to 8.00 a.m.

Immediately on signing, Sky (as the lead partner) applied for approval for the Christian Channel Europe from BT (British Telecom), Astra and the Government of Luxembourg.

And there it simmered.

The middle of August found us still without premises for the fledgling Channel. Europe's potential first daily Christian television network was still operating out of a three-bedroom, three-storey character house in Surrey, a stone's throw from the River Thames, situated immediately behind Hampton Court village.

Our lounge had become the working area. In fact the whole house had turned into a working area! At that stage, we only had one fax machine, one telephone line and had been working avidly at expanding into Hampton Court village or thereabouts, into a two- or three-room office.

However, *every* place we saw that we felt could be utilized turned out, on application for further details, to have just been let – *every* time. We were becoming perplexed. All we wanted was a small office in the local area, and yet every single premises that looked even vaguely suitable was immediately snatched, seemingly from under our very noses, and now we had just six weeks to launch date.

God was about to provide for us again, in the most remarkable way.

A few weeks earlier, I had felt led to phone the Family Channel to ask their marketing department to recommend a good marketing company in the cable and satellite industry. They had recommended a young company based at the Family Channel, which also handled their account.

One sweltering mid-August morning, we arrived at the Family Channel in Maidstone, Kent, had our meeting with the marketing company, and were on our way out, when we were introduced to the marketing director who offered to take us on a five-minute tour of the Family Channel Studios.

Well, what *we* didn't know, but what God surely knew, was that this five-minute tour was to turn into over an hour-and-a-half, and that the Family Channel were planning to rent out some of their studio site to independent cable and satellite channels ... We left that afternoon with a deal on the table for discussion.

By the first week of September, we were resident in the Family

Channel Studios in Maidstone. God had given us the perfect address to launch from – Television Center, Vinters Park, Maidstone.

We were given a section of the first floor as our production offices, an edit suite that was totally locked out to the Christian Channel, sixteen dedicated telephone lines, desks, chairs, a betacam recording machine and access to three studios as and when they were required.

On top of this we had a rent-free period for *all* of the above until January 1996 (which we desperately needed). How wonderful is our God's provision. *God knew* we were truly seeking first His Kingdom, and He added on to us His tremendous provision for the Channel's premises during this crucial launch period. We didn't even *ask* Him for it. This was far and above all we could ask or think!

THEN we found out that it was actually Pat Robertson who owned the Family Channel in England! We hadn't been at all aware of this fact. So we used to write sporadic intense letters to Pat in our early days! Oh, we look back and see so much the hand of God!

Remember, the earlier prophecy that had said in a few days we would stand before two men had also stated that God was bringing us the right buildings and equipment (edit suite).

As a matter of interest, the final element to that prophecy was that there would be yet a third man, of great importance, who would be *right* on time ... Looking back, today, we sit in amazement at how timely our meeting of Albert Dicken was, but more about that later.

Surely God has proven Himself faithful to us time after time. What exciting days we are living in!

CHAPTER TWELVE

FINAL FRONTIER

Well, NOW THE APPLICATION by Sky on the Christian Channel's behalf for the approvals from BT, Astra and the Government of Luxembourg was underway. We gained the approval from BT fairly easily; Astra was a more lengthy process but was agreed by early September but now the Government of Luxembourg started to drag its heels.

Sky had informed us that these approvals were nothing more than a formality. They reassured us that they would take approximately ten days. The application to the Government of Luxembourg had been submitted about eighteen days previously, and still there was no sign of an answer.

The money that was in the escrow account could not be released until we had all three approvals. So, although we had over a hundred thousand pounds ($180,000) launch capital in the escrow account, we quite categorically couldn't touch a penny of it.

It was early September. We had less than twenty days to launch and quite patently, although God had released His funds to us, they

101

were now stuck. We couldn't pay for our design, our marketing or our PR company. We couldn't *even* pay for one run of our launch brochures.

To make it worse – if the Government of Luxembourg for some obscure and satanic reason decided not to grant the Channel approval, *everything* would be lost.

There would be no Christian Channel Europe, no GOD Channel today. *Everything* was now hinging on the Government of Luxembourg.

Now we had another crisis of decision. Should we call all our activities to a halt?

We had already commissioned all our onscreen graphics, our launch brochures, started to edit the first month's programs and received most of our material from Europe and America.

Should we delay our launch *yet* again a month to November?

And finally, if we didn't, would we *dare* to go ahead with our press launch on 27 September?

Suddenly visions loomed of Rory and me standing in front of the London press telling them we didn't actually exist. After all the struggles, all the crises we had been through, we seemed to be up against a rockface.

Remember the grand skeptics, eyes were all fixed on the little upstart David, waiting to see if maybe he *could* just possibly, by some outside chance, be the one to kill Goliath. They had already scoffed at our previous postponement – another one would cause complete disbelief in the camp of observers.

We also sensed that if we put our launch off *again*, all the media buyers would get cold feet and probably decide that we would never launch and possibly withdraw their support. So finally we said, "Father – do you *want* us to postpone till November or to go ahead and launch by faith?"

And God said, "LAUNCH."

And then we said, "Father – do you want us to announce the press conference in London on 27 September?"

And God said, "ANNOUNCE."

We took the longest deep breath we had ever taken, knowing that if we had *not* heard God's voice on this issue, our bones would be fit for the vultures in the field.

And so we worked day by day towards the launch by faith, with no budget, knowing that in the natural, the house could come crashing down around us like a pack of cards.

We started the countdown to the press conference. The twenty-sixth was the final day to cancel. We could not legally go ahead and announce to the country that we were launching unless Sky had the final approval from Luxembourg.

Fifteen days to launch ... no word from Luxembourg.

Ten days to launch ... no word from Luxembourg.

Then, miracle of miracles, five thousand pounds ($8,000) arrived all the way from Pastor Ulf Ekman's church – Word of Life in Uppsala, Sweden. We were so grateful! Five days to launch ... no approvals.

Then it dawned on us – that the State of Luxembourg owns the entire strip of airspace called Astra in Europe. This was surely where the Prince of the Power of the air had his stronghold in Europe. Now we started to realize this was Satan's final bulwark.

It was at this crucial stage that the secular PR company we were working with got extremely nervous. They were arranging our national press conference – would they get paid?

Three days to launch – no approvals. Launch budget still tied up in escrow. Now *we* got extremely nervous – "Hello, God ... Hi! It's Wendy ... it's Rory ... your children ... cough ... ahem ... we seem to have a slight hiccup here ... Earth to Heaven ... SOS!"

The twenty-fifth of September arrived. One day to the press conference ... no approvals.

The twenty-sixth of September ... we were in a graphics studio, cutting the final stage of our audio-visual press presentation together ... no approvals.

Then, late that afternoon, after every boundary of faith had been pushed to the limit ... a fax came through – "THE GOVERNMENT OF LUXEMBOURG APPROVES..."

Glory to God in the highest – the greatest victory in the heavenlies over Luxembourg had been won. Our mighty, powerful God had come through in such splendor. If ever the powers of darkness had wanted to roadblock the move of God, it was *now*. And you know what, dear reader, they couldn't. This was God's television Channel. This was *not* just a good idea. This was *God's* idea and He was jealous over it. *Nothing* would stop His baby from being born.

And so it was that on Wednesday 27 September 1995, we and Pastor Colin Dye, Senior Pastor of Kensington Temple, gathered together in front of the national press in London.

God's baby was about to be born – unscathed, perfectly formed, the parents a bit the worse for wear from the labor, but nothing that a cup of tea and a biscuit couldn't fix!

SOME FAVOURITE PICTURES FROM OUR FAMILY ALBUM

My father –
the very dashing Hal "Doc."

My mother –
a young Jean.

Rory's father, Bob Stephen, and mother, Lona.

Our wonderful children –
Christian and Samantha.

Signing with BSkyB in June 1995.

The Dedication Service in April 1996, when we dedicated the
Christian Channel to God. Praying for us along with Benny Hinn,
are Ulf Ekman and Colin Dye.

Rory with Derek and Ruth Prince who are now both with Jesus in Heaven.

Rory in Africa with our wonderful Mr and Mrs Dicken.

Rory and Wendy interviewing the late Ed Cole
on *Friday Night Live* in England.

Rory and me in our first transmission suite
in Newcastle, England.

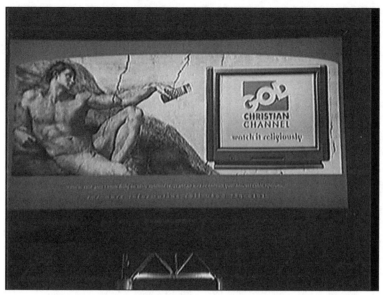

The "Michaelangelo" advert
on billboards across London.

We are no strangers to controversy and the road is tough:
our billboard campaign really put God into focus.

Emma Owen, formerly of the leading UK Christian band, *The Tribe*, who is one of the presenters of GOD TV's youth flagship program, *Dream On TV*.

Dream studio with Linz and group.

Dream on TV's ever-popular Jennifer Hughes,
who is a well-known face on many different GOD TV programs
and LIVE broadcasts.

David Aldous interviewing Mahesh and Bonnie Chavda
for *In Depth*.

With Pat Robertson on the *700 Club* at Virginia Beach.

With Evander Holyfield on the *Rory & Wendy Show*.

With Benny Hinn on Mission's Week.

Broadcasting to the world
from our new
broadcast center
in Jerusalem.

Our fantastic team
in the UK.

Bo Sanders, Rory Alec, Thomas Robinson, Pauline Wong
and Ronnie Sit.

Taking Hong Kong for Jesus.

Our GOD TV teams across the world

Scandanavian team.

Florida team.

Washington DC team.

Our GOD TV teams across the world

Israel
team.

India
team.

South Africa
team.

Christian and Samantha
in front of the Statue of Liberty.

Christian and Samantha
on boat in front of New York skyline.

Christian at Christmas.

Rory with Christian at Niagra Falls.

Our dog.

Writing *Fall of Lucifer*
in Fredricksburg, Virginia.

An informal shot of Rory and me as part of the launch
of the *Rory & Wendy Show*.

CHAPTER THIRTEEN

FACING THE PRESS

I T WAS WEDNESDAY MORNING, 27 September. There, seated facing the press in the Cumberland Hotel, Mayfair were myself, Rory and Pastor Colin Dye – the innocents about to be thrown to the wolves!

We had approached Colin months before when we quite patently had nothing. He had listened patiently and very politely to our dreams of a Christian television channel but we must admit that we had left slightly disheartened, not knowing if we had managed to impart the vision effectively.

However, just over a fortnight later, we received the most heart-warming, marvelous letter from Pastor Colin, saying that he had prayed about our request for him to be on our Council of Reference and that God had spoken to him. He had a great conviction that God was with us, would consider it a privilege to be a part of what God was clearly involved in and would assist us in any way possible.

Through the rocky times during our initial launch period Colin was a consistent source of great wisdom and encouragement and has become a trusted friend. (We do so enjoy his company!) We honor him for the commitment that he has shown not only to GOD TV, but to Rory and myself personally.

Anyway, so there were the three of us facing the pack of wolves: *European Broadcast News*, *The Guardian*, *The Times* to name but a few.

One particular photographer in the front row was staring at us as if we had come off Noah's ark itself. In fact, he kept staring throughout our whole presentation in a rather disconcerting manner as though we were from another planet.

I think that the journalists were prepared for some sort of cross between *Songs of Praise*, Jimmy Swaggart and the local choral evensong. Instead the showreel started with DC Talk and contemporary Christian music. *That* blew a few of the religious cobwebs away!

Then there was the unmistakable lady in red – religious correspondent for a particular newspaper – who was to become a long-term challenger of GOD TV.

After the initial press interviews had been conducted, it was time for the photographs. There was an attempt to get Rory and me to stand on chairs against a backdrop of a little girl with JESUS written on a bandana around her forehead and Rory refused, visualizing headlines "Christian Channel brainwashes your children." When we saw the scathing output of certain journalists (especially the one in red) we were relieved that he had taken that stand. God bless the secular press.

Then it was time for BBC Radio Five Live which Rory and Colin conducted, also VIVA Radio and then onto the regional radio stations – BBC Radio Northampton, BBC Lines, BBC Derby, BBC Scotland, BBC Suffolk, BBC Kent, BBC Newcastle, BBC Wilts, BBC Southern Counties, BBC Lancaster and BBC York.

That night news of the impending launch of the Christian Channel was broadcast across Europe on EBN (European Business

News) and RAI (Italian State Television), and also on Austrian television.

Now we had three days to go until our first broadcast. All systems go!

Rory and I were buried in the edit suite from morning till midnight, overseeing the cutting together of the programs, putting together the final television formats, and directing the Channel's operations frantically from the "black hole"!

Then came a phone call from Peter Stremes, of Telewest Broadband, who we had tried to persuade a year earlier to take the Channel. He had seen us on European Broadcast News the previous evening. He would send us a contract.

God was amazing! This was the biggest cable operator in the United Kingdom and they had approached us before we even launched.

The phone continued to be jammed with enquirers, critics, enthusiasts and an incessant stream of requests for radio and television interviews.

Our staff was growing day by day at a rapid rate. This was because we took brief respite from our "black hole" at intervals to recruit the people we needed, interviewing all types, including some rather "strange" Steven Spielberg enthusiasts, among others … some of these stayed! I will be kind and not incriminate them except to say that it was the first and only time that I ever saw our scheduler in a black suit and tie (he looked remarkably like a funeral director!). In fact we were getting quite crammed by now, working frantically for our launch on Sunday 1st October.

Friday 29 September dawned – this was Rory's thirtieth birthday. The edit suite was visited with a birthday cake (quickly purchased from the local supermarket) and he dutifully endured "Happy Birthday" sung by the now rather motley, but very enthusiastic, if not slightly off-key, Christian Channel crew!

Saturday came and went and we were still frantically editing. The tapes just got couriered to Sky in time for the deadline.

And so, at five o'clock in the morning on Sunday the first of October, as soon as the Sci Fi Channel signed off, the Christian Channel logo appeared for the first time on Transponder 47 across nineteen nations in Europe.

The Sunday papers were bought in a great flurry that day ... especially *The Independent on Sunday* (several of our fervent supporters, including my mother, raided about ten copies from the local corner shop!), which had run a three-page color spread in their color magazine section that morning.

I have to say that although Peter Popham's article was at times scathing, it was *certainly* entertaining reading! After citing Benny Hinn, Kenneth and Gloria Copeland, to name but a few, Popham wrote: *"Such stuff is not going to help an Anglican rector's cornflakes go down, but there is little doubt that it will find an audience."* He certainly did his homework, except for one glaring error where he cited Gerald Coates as our pastor in Esher. Not true. We had lived in Esher, though. Popham continued:

American television audiences have been subjected to such hysterical blandishments for years. But in Britain, religious television still means the sober proprieties of Songs of Praise.

The established churches are still bitterly opposed to the opening up of Britain to an influx of televangelism, and so, as a pre-emptive strike against it, had planned to launch in the spring of next year a cable channel, Ark 2.

Backed by the Church of England, the Catholics, the Methodists and other denominations, it will present the safe, responsible, balanced face of mainstream British Christianity.

Now their plans have been spoiled. Two young, charismatic

125

Christians have come out of nowhere and accomplished the thing the churches dreaded the most.

They have enabled the televangelists to get a foot inside British television's door. Their names are Rory and Wendy Alec, born-again Christians who arrived in the UK from South Africa four years ago. Their baby is Christian Channel Europe (CCE) and it arrives on British screens by courtesy of Astra, the television satellite company.

He continued (at least he called us charming ... to make up for the other two and a half pages of descriptions that weren't quite so flattering!):

"The Alecs are charming, but even before transmission began, they had incurred the wrath of the religious establishment. The sweetly reasonable Ernest Rea, head of religious broadcasting at the BBC, said, 'It's a very unwelcome development. British evangelists' – presumably those within the mainstream – 'have very clearly decided not to repeat the US televangelist experience – not to exploit the vulnerability of viewers – not to proselytise overtly.'"

Well, on and on it went. Popham did mention however, that *"Starting from small independent churches, South Africa's religious revival has grown so fast and so far that it has touched every denomination in the country."* And then, as though we were about to beam up a strange brand of Afrikaner neo-Nazi propaganda over Britain, he stated, *"Young, gifted and fanatical, the Alecs are its perfect exemplars."*

During the next few days of our launch period, interviews were conducted with Talk Radio UK, BBC Radio 4 Sunday, ITV Meridian and BBC Radio World Service.

We then had a call inviting Rory onto *Newsnight* with Jon Snow. This was canceled just an hour before, due an overriding story, which broke from Gibraltar.

Articles appeared in *The Guardian, The Evening Standard, The Observer,* and *The Daily Mail,* and throughout the regional print media and the media trade press. The headlines that week included *"All rise for dawn chorus", "TV blessings from on high", "Do not convert your dish", "Heavens above!", "Tele-evangelism comes to Britain"* and *"Breakfast with God!"*

One London publication even warned the "purveyors of erotica" to *"watch out for the new Christian Channel as its statement of faith promises eternal damnation for the unrepentant sinner!"*

Then we were approached by BBC1 and invited onto *Good Morning with Anne and Nick* scheduled for early November. During this time, we were also approached by the senior editor of BBC1's *Everyman* documentary program who was interested in producing a fifty-minute documentary on the Christian Channel Europe.

I quote from the BBC's letter to us:

"It is our job to inform the public of important developments to the religious scene and it is now our belief that your venture is such a development and could well change the religious land-scape of Europe of the future."

During this time period, we were still spending eighteen-hour days in the edit suite overseeing the Channel's output. Meanwhile, back in administration, the main focus became setting up the computers to handle the response that had started to flood into the ministry.

In between this, Rory started to visit churches in Scotland, Ireland, Germany and Sweden. The Body of Christ were fast becoming aware of the Christian Channel's existence and were excited!

Unhappy subscribers to cable were starting to demand the

Christian Channel and suddenly we were receiving calls from cable operators nationwide asking for proposals and contracts.

Christian Music Television was starting to take off and was becoming a huge hit with the young people around Europe.

It was now late October and we had to give the BBC an answer as to whether or not we would go ahead with the *Everyman* documentary.

We now had first-hand experience of the secular press, so we prayed very seriously about our involvement in *Everyman*, but we felt that God said, "Yes." We met with the producer Chris Mann and agreed to a shooting schedule in early November. Part of this agreement involved allowing Chris Mann's crew to film us during our trip to Birmingham to appear on the *Anne and Nick show*. So there we were in Birmingham, not only about to appear on a major UK magazine program at the time, (which was intimidating enough), but we had the BBC1 *Everyman* crew following every movement.

Before we went live, we had an excellent conversation about Christian values and Anne Diamond's concern about the adverts for the Playboy Channel being flighted on Sky. Unfortunately, as our promo video was rolled in, I saw Anne's eyes start to bulge in a rather, "This is Bible-bashing fundamentalism ... what have we got here?" expression.

So, from the warm, expansive attitude she had previously shown, she did become slightly more on guard, but Nick continued, undeterred. All went smoothly except, as the *Everyman* documentary revealed (God bless you, Chris Mann) my false fingernail flew off in Nick's face just as we closed!

But the most amazing outcome of the *Anne and Nick show* was the actual telephone response of the viewers. On the show, the producers allowed just two responses out – one for Christian television and one against. Behind the scenes they had, in that short space of time, one hundred and four telephone calls from the public.

One hundred *for* Christian television in Britain and only *four* against. How I wish the world had known *that* fact! God's people were excited!

November continued in a flurry of activity, visiting churches, preparing marketing proposals, sourcing new programs, expanding our cable penetration, sending out mail-shots. Eventually, we distributed more than one hundred and eighty thousand brochures across Britain and mainland Europe.

Meanwhile, the BBC1 crew were still avidly filming our progress. They filmed us moving into the house in Maidstone, Rory visiting Ulf Ekman's church in Uppsala, Sweden, where GOD TV has always received a fantastic welcome; they even filmed us stirring soup over the stove. In fact, our lives became theirs for most of November.

The airing date for the documentary called *The Miracle Channel* was scheduled for 28 January 1996 and the flack began.

The Morning Star labeled us as *"fundamentalist, Bible-bashing"* and *"a disturbing phenomenon"* (*The Morning Star*, London, 27 January), while *The Observer* proclaimed that the Channel *"preaches hell fire to sinners, material prosperity for believers, and targets vulnerable young viewers"* (The *Observer*, London, 28 January).

The Sunday Times stated:

"Strangely for Everyman, *no questions are asked, no debate raised. It is in fact a free puff for Rory and Wendy who are filmed as 'blessed' parents at home, and as 'blessed' presenters at work on a Channel where people claim to be 'genuinely excited by what God is doing', as if he were the new Tarantino."*

The Financial Times declared:

"Everyman on BBC reveals what a flap Rory and Wendy Alec have caused in the dovecoat of religious broadcasting."

The Newcastle Evening Chronicle warned:

> *"Keep your head down, lock the doors and pull out the TV plug – the telly evangelists are at the door. And judging by last Sunday's* Everyman *on BBC1 we need all the protection we can gather. Fifty minutes of what was in effect an unchallenged promotion of Christian Television was frightening."*

And of course, *The Times* did mention that Rory and I were *"brain dead"*, God bless them.

Well, we were able to watch a preview of the documentary three days before it went out across Great Britain.

We had been filmed answering our critics' comments in the final *Everyman* interview by the producer Chris Mann, who afterwards aired a genuine relief that we seemed only mildly shaken by the overt criticism. (We had actually been prepared for far, *far* worse!)

I have to confess that when we actually viewed our two most scathing critics on camera, Ernest Rea (Head of Religious Programing, BBC) and A. Gill, TV Critic for *The Sunday Times*, I found both, although at times apoplectic in their condemnation of the Channel and on occasion remarkably scathing, to be sincere men.

And in Ernest Rea's defense, he had, after the actual broadcast of the documentary, called us "genuinely sincere," although he did add that we were in a "spiritual cocoon."

The *Everyman* documentary was aired on Sunday 28 January and the reaction was incredible! The Christian Channel phones rang off the hook!

There was also an interesting and heated response to the BBC. Here are some of the comments quoted from their Factual Unit report:

> *"A marvelous program."*

"Complained the program came across as mere propaganda for the couple featured."

"Thanks the BBC for showing the power of God!"

"Felt the program gave too much publicity to Christian Television."

"Felt it was a very good, impartial, fair and very interesting program."

"It was a very lopsided and anti-view on the Christian Channel Europe."

"Absolutely excellent. I support everything the program was depicting."

"Said the BBC ought to take a leaf out of the Channel's book."

(I'm sure that probably turned the long-suffering Mr Rea a shade of puce!)

One comment that I really enjoyed was a pastor who phoned the BBC to say that *"John Wesley was 'laughed at' when he first founded the Methodist Church, so the critics of the Christian Channel are used to it!"*

Then the Christian Channel was featured on the BBC program *Right to Reply*, where again the increasingly tormented Mr Rea was taken to task by one of the BBC's born-again viewers on the attitude he displayed to the Christian Channel on the documentary.

All in all, we were pleasantly surprised by the treatment that the BBC gave the Channel.

You see, we have *never ever* taken the press seriously. And we never will. The only press we take seriously is the press release from our heavenly Father. It is what He says that counts.

Yes – of course they call us heretics, Bible bashers, fundamentalists. They called Jesus a lunatic! The religious spirits across Europe were *howling* with rage.

Somehow, someway, two thousand years ago the devil, looking for a king who would be born to power, riches and influence, let the Son of God, born in a humble stable, slip through his hands, and so it was the same with GOD TV; the devil had let the infant Christian Channel Europe slip through his hands and he was *enraged*.

He had been looking for those with money and power and earthly sway, for those are *his* yardstick. You see, dear reader, the one thing that literally confounds the devil is the anointing.

For God chooses whom He will choose and whereas Satan's basis for choosing is natural strength and ability, God's list of "who's who" is based on those He has foreordained to serve Him from the beginning of time. It is also based on a willing and available heart, on His calling and His anointing.

God chose Moses the stutterer, David the shepherd boy and even His own Son was born of a humble carpenter. And His criteria have never changed. For what God holds more precious than gold is our total surrender – for surely, friends, He looks at our hearts.

CHAPTER FOURTEEN

THE EUROTHON

W E WERE NOW FACED with an interesting situation. From the first of October, we had thirty-four thousand pounds' ($55,000) worth of revenue coming in every month, but our overheads (at the bare minimum) added up to approximately eighty-seven thousand pounds a month ($140,000), leaving us with a monthly deficit of over fifty thousand pounds ($85,000). That added up to approximately 840,000 pounds a year ($1.5million). Oh, we look back on that with longing nowadays. As I write, our yearly overheads add up to *over thirty million dollars!*

God had told us to launch by faith and we were being obedient. But we had some distinct disadvantages that were continually threatening our survival. Firstly, we were a brand new ministry and therefore had no partner base, launching into Christian television, which was completely uncharted territory in Europe.

Where churches already *had* their own equipment, or were starting to fund it, we as the first daily Christian television Channel in

Western Europe, had to *hire* our equipment for every shoot at exorbitant prices.

In America, Christian TV's financial needs are met by holding *telethons*, which is where the running costs of television are put before the viewers and an ongoing appeal is made for up to a week to support the work of God through the broadcast media.

Now, in Europe there were two obstacles.

First, we were, under *no* circumstances and on *no* condition, allowed to appeal for funds on air, under ITC regulations. (This later changed for GOD TV in October 2002, when the GOD Channel was awarded a new broadcast license in Spain giving us greater freedom, not only to raise funds on air, but to make a clear stand for what we believe with regard to a number of issues.)

Second, because of just an unfortunate few excesses and misuses in America, fund-raising had become such a contentious issue in Europe – one we wanted to steer well clear of, for the time being.

But *what* were we to do? *How* would we survive? Media ministries were plummeting all around us at an alarming rate, through lack of funds. They were *all* struggling and seemed to be issuing unending pleas for finance.

Why God always seemed to call us to the impossible only He knows! You see, every step that we have taken, only God has been able to bring us through.

We were not starting small, as all the big Christian television networks had started off in America and grown. For example, CBN started with one small station in Charlotte; TBN started with one station in Los Angeles.

Here we were, starting off by God's grace with access to the *whole* of Western Europe – nineteen nations – on the most exclusive European satellite, with airtime immediately taking us into the big league costing thousands of pounds, combined with television over-heads which aren't "Mickey Mouse."

The UK's Channel 5 launch budget was reported to have been two hundred million pounds. Ours was one hundred and sixteen thousand pounds. And it was gobbled up almost on our first day.

As the Christian Channel, we had in an incredibly short space of time grown an amazing family of thousands right across Europe – growing at a rapid rate every single day – but the last thing we wanted to do to all of our new excited viewers was to ask for money! Rory and I were adamant: we didn't want our new family of viewers to feel pressurized to give.

But things were becoming desperate. How would we survive through Christmas?

Then we received a phone call. Claude and Freeda Bowers were coming to London – to visit Harrods and to shop. Now this time, we could hear in Claude's voice, he really meant *shop!*

Two weeks before Christmas, Claude, Freeda and the Super-channel 55 team arrived in London. First stop, the Christian Channel. After dinner together, Rory approached Claude about holding a "Eurothon."

Let me explain. When we had been in America the previous year on our disastrous trip, Rory and I had stared wide-eyed at four in the morning, watching Paul Crouch, of America's largest Christian television network, ask his viewers to support the work of Christian television financially.

We had stared at each other, open-mouthed.

What if *we* could hold a telethon, not in Europe, but in America, where people understood the tremendous power of Christian television and the influence that it could carry? Where the people had a heart for missions and would see the urgency of getting the Gospel out to the dark continent ... Europe. We wouldn't call it a telethon ... we would call it a *Eurothon.*

Claude and Rory met for breakfast the next morning. Once

again, God had lured Claude out to Britain to "shop" and dumped on him!

God bless you, Claude, for your obedience to the prompting of the Lord. We honor you for your unhesitating willingness to hear God when He spoke to you.

Claude, unbeknown to us, was conducting his own television channel's telethon for a week starting on 3 January. He had already planned a night on the following Monday where he would raise funds for Europe and Haiti.

It could easily dovetail. On his return to America, Claude would approach the other independent Christian television station owners and see if they would each be prepared to link up through America for one night to raise funds from their viewers for the Christian Channel.

"Oh!" we said brightly, "what about Benny Hinn being our special guest?"

Claude stared at us slightly skeptically!

And so, over Christmas, we waited, totally at peace that this was the Lord's Channel, not knowing if the Eurothon would happen; then towards the end of December, we received a call from Claude – the Eurothon was on.

Now, if you cast your mind back to our first disastrous trip to America, you will remember that in prophecy God had said that we would find great favor with the men we would meet and we had deduced that great favor equaled money.

Well, Claude had returned and approached every one of the men that we had met on our previous seemingly futile trip to America who owned a major independent Christian television station and asked these same men if they would get involved in the Eurothon, and, wait for God's favor. Saints – *every single man had agreed to co-host the Christian Channel Eurothon. That* first trip had come to fruition in *God's time*, not *our time* – nearly nine months later.

Oh, how disillusioned and disappointed we get when God's plan seems to come to nought, only to find that He, in His magnificent overview has it all *meticulously* planned far better than we can ever dream, hope or imagine! What a miracle-working God we serve!

Jerry Rose of WCFC Chicago, Marcus Lamb of KMTX TV 29, Dallas, Garth Kuns of WTCT Channel 27, Illinois and Russ and Norma Bixler of Cornerstone TV 40, Pittsburgh, had *all* agreed to devote at least three hours of their prime Saturday night airtime to the Christian Channel Europe. Claude Bowers in Orlando, would host the Eurothon and ... wait for it, friends ... Pastor Benny Hinn had agreed to take time out from his hectic schedule to be our special guest that evening.

Oh – the goodness of God towards us – what delight He has in watching His children believe for the impossible.

And you know, God actually had to slap our wrists the week before we left and say, "Get in faith for the money, kids!" Because we had almost over-learnt our lesson and were saying, "Whatever God wants – it's up to Him."

So now we felt we had His *permission* to believe, we roused ourselves, and started to believe for two hundred thousand pounds ($350,000) to be raised in America. And so, on 6 January, we boarded a Virgin flight to Orlando and were about to enter one of the most exciting weeks of our lives.

CHAPTER FIFTEEN

THIS WAS OUR DAY!

AS THE VIRGIN AIRLINER drew nearer to Florida, there was a definite change in the spiritual climate and we felt a great anticipation. We were not to be disappointed.

We were picked up, taken to the hotel where we were to rest and told we'd be collected the following morning to attend the ten o'clock service at the World Outreach Center, Pastor Benny Hinn's church.

Well, it was as though we walked into a tidal wave of blessing. Oh, how wonderful it was to bask in the anointing of God. All through the Sunday and Monday, there was a very real presence of Almighty God surrounding us. We laid our heads down on the pillow in blessing. We woke up to more blessing. Next, we were taken shopping!

Janice, a member of the World Outreach Center, had been led by the Lord to buy Rory a whole new wardrobe and Freeda was buying me one too! What generous-hearted people.

This was *incredible!* Suddenly everywhere we looked was abundance and blessing.

You have to understand that for over four years we had been living in a place called "Paying the Price" and there had been no luxuries. I had literally worn one pair of favored comfortable boots through two winters; my favorite trousers were on their last legs; my make-up was almost finished; my perfume bottles were empty; and I had one pair of earrings.

Rory was in the same situation because the only thing that mattered was to launch Christian television into Europe, not to look like an advert for a designer brand!

But it seemed as if God was literally determined to bless us. I cannot tell you what it was like to suddenly have a beautiful watch and lovely earrings, to have my favorite "Estee" perfume and some gorgeous clothes! And there was Rory with new apparel, looking like a young up-and-coming preacher.

God was blessing us to fulfill His purpose. He was about to launch us into a phase of ministry, where we would be sharing from platforms all across Europe and America, where we would be speaking at churches and conventions, be interviewed by the press and generally be in both the public and secular eye. So we needed to put our best foot forward.

We woke up, again surrounded by the presence of God – this was our day – the Christian Channel Eurothon! Late that afternoon, we were still editing together the inserts for that evening. Frantically we changed into our Eurothon attire, our make-up was applied ... and the opening credits started to roll.

Claude Bowers introduced Marcus Lamb and Russ and Norma Bixler who had flown in from Dallas and Pittsburgh respectively for the evening's events. Some leading ministers had all pre-taped enthusiastic and supportive messages encouraging America to support the Channel both in prayer and financially.

Our clips of British and European News were aired and then we were introduced.

And the telephones started to ring.

And they rang ... and they rang ... in fact, for at least an hour, there wasn't a single telephone that wasn't ringing. America was excited.

Then at eight-thirty, special guest Pastor Benny Hinn arrived.

And the phones rang ... and they rang pledging a thousand dollars ... seventy dollars ... a thousand dollars ... sixty ... fifty ... a thousand ... and on and on ... Pastor Benny had to leave by ten o'clock, but he very kindly promised the viewers that he would pray over all the pledges the next morning in church. By the end of the evening over two hundred and fifty thousand dollars had been pledged to the development of the Christian Channel Europe.

We serve an amazing God.

We fell into bed exhausted but exhilarated – I'm sure we slept with beaming smiles on our faces that night (of relief). God in His great compassion had opened a way where it seemed there was no way and made His face to shine upon us.

CHAPTER SIXTEEN

GOOD MORNING
EUROPE!

I HAD STAYED sipping cappuccinos in Starbucks in America a little too long, because I have to admit that as the plane veered through the gray murky clouds nearing Heathrow on that Monday morning, I was very tempted to get a calling to Orlando in the winter and California in summer and take the next plane back to America.

Instead, I descended the aeroplane steps and followed Rory reluctantly into the Heathrow terminal with the distinctly growing sensation that we were about to re-enter "Hellsville" and the spiritual frontline in Europe.

Once we were back on British soil, we were bombarded by what seemed to be a hundred varying pieces of information. We also walked straight into the aftermath of the BBC's controversial documentary, on us entitled "The Miracle Channel," which had been broadcast two weeks earlier, not to mention the articles that circulated in the British press about Benny Hinn's million-dollar faith injection.

The Sunday Mirror wanted to interview us for an article to appear in the Easter edition of their color magazine supplement. (The front cover of the 7 April issue later read *"And in the beginning there was the Good Book. Then cameth the strumming of guitars and those that fainteth in the aisle. Now Christian TV hath arrived and we ask of the multitude: who shall cast the first stone?"*)

We had been invited to appear on Selina Scott's talk show on NBC Superchannel.

We were due to be interviewed by Jonathan King of London's Talk Radio. We had also seemingly been taken to task by the more traditional Christian channel Ark 2, who were seemingly using Ernest Rea's (Head of Religious Broadcasting BBC) comments about us from *Everyman*, as a tool to convince the media that compared to us (the Christian Channel), the American televangelists (overt evangelism, Pentecostalism) were as harmless as a pet hamster. We were portrayed more as a rabid alligator!

But now it was back to settling down to the day-to-day running of the Channel and straight away into filming the next series of *Good Morning Europe*.

And therein lies a tale.

In the initial months of the Channel's launch, Rory and I had been avoiding appearing *in front* of the camera, but there had been a nagging feeling, which grew stronger each day, that God actually wanted us in front of the camera and not just directing operations from behind the scenes.

But we kept suppressing the Holy Spirit's gentle nudging.

However, by the beginning of December, person after person kept coming to us with a word from the Lord that we should be communicating with our viewers on a program of our own.

Finally, George Otis (a well-known pioneer of radio in the Christian world) who was visiting with us, spoke to us quite emphatically about it, not knowing that we were dragging our heels.

There was no doubt about it – we were being disobedient to the next stage in God's plan. We might have to start in a simple way but start we must. And although it was not the way we would have chosen naturally to shoot *Good Morning Europe*, because of our production house background and our aspiration to excellence for the Gospel, we wanted this to be the house that the Lord built, not just our own good idea.

And that is how *Good Morning Europe* started in *our dining room!*

On 25 December, sitting on a borrowed sofa (ours was slightly older), the hired camera rolled and so we started *Good Morning Europe with Rory and Wendy Alec.*

Now, as our viewers no doubt noticed, Rory took to being in front of the camera like a duck to water, but without fail, I would *clam* up every time! When we played the tape of our first few *Good Morning Europe* programs to my father, he looked at me suspiciously. Apart from looking like a clone of Morticia Adams with big hair! – (my rapidly entering teenage son is totally mortified at any visuals of my earlier state) – my first welcome to the viewers was so *austere* that it would have terrified the living daylights out of me if I had been on the receiving end.

"What's the matter with you?" My Father stared at me in a strange fashion. "It looks as if all the life's drained out of you!" He then proceeded (with a grand twinkle in his eye) to call me "Dumbo" (as in dumb brunette!) the entire weekend, not able to believe how his normally vibrant daughter could appear so totally devoid of life on *Good Morning Europe.*

Well, they say you get used to cameras, and day by day, I started to relax ... sometimes we relax too much!

Then after Christmas, we decided to move to the dining-room table, which seemed to work quite well, but we still only had one camera which, adept as our cameraman was, proved to be quite inhibiting.

Those were raw early days of production, but what fun times we had ... from Rory catching me still chewing gum as the camera rolled ... the mobile phone accidentally being left on the table for half the program ... Then there was the time when our cat gaily walked through the open door and wouldn't stop miaowing.

Then there was the morning when we were starting our introductions and I kept bursting into giggles. It was getting *so* bad, that Rory was actually starting to get quite mad at me ... quite mad continuing into really mad as we reached the sixth take.

"It's the Holy Spirit!" I spluttered.

Well, from Rory's expression, it was quite evident that he was not at all amused.

"It *is* the Holy Spi ... " Another hysterical gale of laughter.

Rory was sitting there, completely furious. (Later he had to repent.)

For indeed God, if we surrender to Him, moves in ways that may be foolishness to the natural mind, but the end result is life for the people. On that particular morning, as on many mornings afterwards, God wanted to reach out and touch His people who were suffering from depression, to lift those who were bowed down.

You see God didn't want *Good Morning Europe* to be an entertainment show – He wanted to meet the needs of our viewers and to interact with them. He wanted us to share with our wonderful and rapidly growing family across the nations. This is something we have always kept in mind as we have developed a whole range of LIVE programing over the years, including *Behind the Screens*, *Friday Night Live* and lately *The Rory and Wendy Show*. We are not called to "play television," but to minister to the needs of God's people. When you see Rory and me live on television, apart from sharing with you the excitement of all that is going on through the ministry of GOD TV, our goal is to meet whatever need you may have as a viewer.

We're there to pray for our viewers, to stand with you, to welcome you as part of our family and to reach the Body of Christ across the globe – all standing in the gap together. Through all the letters and e-mails we receive, we are so aware that there are so many of our precious viewers who are struggling – those who watch us from council flats, on income support, battling with the hardship of day-to-day life; there are those who have just been told they have only a few months to live by the doctors; those desperate for freedom from addictions, and habits they can't seem to get victory over on their own; and there are those who are hurting, lonely and rejected.

Let us never make the mistake of playing television ... for the Lord is consumed with the welfare of His people. They are top priority on His list and whenever we go too long without praying on screen, He gently whispers to us, "Meet the needs of MY people."

Well, on our return from America, we arrived back to over a thousand letters from our extended European family, so excited and enthused with what God was doing.

From Slovakia, Lithuania, Germany, Poland, Switzerland, Austria, Sweden, Norway, Denmark, Italy, Spain, Estonia, Holland, England, Scotland, Ireland, Portugal ... the letters flooded in.

The testimonies of salvation, of healing, of the Holy Spirit overcoming our viewers, of our viewers' absolute joy at being a part of the Christian Channel family! And the literally thousands of letters keep coming in to GOD TV through the years to this day!

Then there was the occasion when we decided to have a "Family" Program as so many of our viewers (mostly our dear viewing grandmothers) who had written in requesting to see our children. So, like a good "House on the Prairie" Alec Family, we

145

dressed Christian (nineteen months) and Samantha (nearly five-years-old) suitably for the grand occasion and proceeded to sit at the dining room table with the camera rolling.

Apart from Christian continuing to repeat "Daddy" rapidly all through Rory's introduction, things were going well. Then he kept waving at the cameramen. Still passable. Then he proceeded to issue the strangest set of what could, at a long shot, be passed as laughter, but sounded more like a pig snorting. Christian has never laughed like that before ... or ever since ... but he did that day!

Now, as a mother, I thought that this was the cutest, adorable thing imaginable but Rory had other ideas.

Christian then proceeded to dismantle one of our artificial roses right in front of the whole of Europe. Scenario – Christian pulls rose head off. Rory is addressing viewers (slightly agitated).

Christian lets out another unbelievable set of snorting. I try not to giggle. Rory is still addressing viewers (extremely irritated with us) not surprisingly as it becomes inordinately difficult for him to concentrate.

Christian pulls stalk of artificial flower in half.

Another long drawn out set of snorting laughter.

I collapse into giggles.

Rory is now furious.

Christian is unceremoniously banned from the set.

Mother is now extremely upset at darling sweet son being expelled.

One gone ... one to go.

We start again.

Samantha does her bit really nicely.

"Good Morning Europe – God loves you." In perfect *House on the Prairie* angelic Christian daughter style.

Then she is instructed to sit quietly while we finish the program.

Meanwhile, I am now *really* upset that Christian has been

banned for snorting and dismantling the flower ... but I still have to smile because we are on TV. I am not a good pretender and the smile is rather wilted.

Then Rory starts to pray.

There is a strange, indefinable bouncing sound. (Whoops.) Samantha is bouncing from sofa to sofa to our left.

Now, I wonder if Samantha is going to be banned too.

Rory continues praying, with furtive glances out of the corner of his eye.

The furtive glances become more ominous.

The camera stops rolling as Rory gives a stern warning to Samantha to desist in the bouncing.

The camera rolls once more and Rory continues to pray for our viewers.

Strange strains of attempted off-key singing filter towards us from the bouncing sofa area intermingled with more bouncing sounds as Rory continues to pray in front of Europe.

Is that smoke that I see billowing out of Rory's ears?

"CUUUTTT!"

The camera stops rolling and Samantha stops rolling as well!

She is now banished – sent up to bed unceremoniously.

Loud wails and sobbing come wafting down the staircase.

Rory looks at me (much happier) and says as the cameras roll "Wendy, pray!"

Rory is now much happier but Wendy is much unhappier at both her poor helpless little darlings' expulsions (even though Rory was right).

I am inspirational – How can I *pray*??

However – after a cup of coffee, a lot of deep breathing and five minutes break, things were back on track, apart from my extremely feeble and insipid smile throughout the whole next program.

You see, we're just a normal family (well our kids might

question that!) called by God coping with the pressures of ministry, family and running a television channel ... and the one thing you'll always know about Rory and Wendy is *what you see is what you get!*

And our viewers are so real too! Oh, they bless us so by their warmth and enthusiasm. We meet many of them at crusades and conventions. In fact at the Benny Hinn Crusade in London and at the Kenneth Copeland Believers' Convention, we were nearly over-run by our viewers! We were brought cheese from Holland, chocolate from Switzerland, postcards, hand-made gifts ... one morning even a bouquet of beautiful flowers arrived from Jersey. (Thank you for that wonderful thought – I never was able to find out who they were from.)

And Rory and I are committed to our viewers. The purity of heart and the hunger for God to be found in Britain and Europe at this time is incredible. It is God's time for revival, and revival starts in the hearts of people like Rory and myself and of each one of our GOD TV family watching each morning in their living rooms.

And together as the Bride of Christ, all the flames shall burn fervently across the nations of this world as a sign and a wonder to this last generation.

What a privilege and an awesome responsibility.

T W E N T Y - F O U R   H O U R S
–   T H E   F I G H T   W A S   O N !

A FTER GREAT WRESTLING in the spirit realm, on 1 September 1997, The Christian Channel's broadcasts were finally extended by BSkyB from three hours in graveyard time every morning, to what was for us a ground-breaking seven hours, from 4.00 a.m. to 11.00 a.m. every day!

With great rejoicing, the Christian Channel was re-branded as "The GOD Channel" – with a billboard and bus campaign across London, England. "Bold, you might say?" "Much too bold," said some of our harsher critics. Ah! But what a reason we had!

Because we had started broadcasting on Britain's major satellite platform, SKY. We were accessible to over twenty-five percent of UK television households, free-to-air, each morning, which meant there were thousands of unchurched people who could easily "stumble" across our programs as they flicked through their channels.

However, our big Christian Channel Europe (CCE) logo on-screen made no sense at all to any channel surfers. We realized that when people are desperate or suicidal and are channel hopping, we had only ONE opportunity to draw their attention.

And it was with this in mind, that while Rory was away in Australia pursuing distribution opportunities for the Channel, I was saying to the Lord – "Father – what is YOUR logo?"

... Batman has a "logo" Superman has a "logo" and I felt that the Father said that we were to put up HIS Name boldly – the Name of the Father – as GOD. Well, I drew the logo that you currently see on your screen today and faxed it over to Rory in Australia, who nearly fell off his chair! But we both sensed that we had the permission of the Holy Spirit and of the Father to broadcast His Name.

And so it was that the GOD logo was birthed, God's television channel branded by the Name of the Father Himself. And NOW when channel hoppers brought us up on screen, they were left in no doubt as to where they were.

The GOD logo on screen was to be a lifeline for the desperate and hurting – a bold statement to the skeptics and curious and a refuge for the needy. The prophetic evangelistic mandate on GOD TV is both an abrasion to the religious and the humanists and a wake-up call to both the Church and the world. And so the Christmas of 1997 saw them woken up with slogans like "Virgin Television," "God is on our side," "Breakfast with God" (breakfast time viewing) and other fairly provocative straplines including "God the Father, God the Son ... and God the TV channel." (As we have grown a little wiser through the years and with hindsight, we would probably have retracted this one. We couldn't fit the third section, "God the Holy Spirit" on the billboard and tried to emphasize our point by giving "god the tv channel" a small "g"!)

Well, it certainly stirred things up. The bishops came out in force especially as there was one enormous poster of a semi-naked Michelangelo right near the gates of Lambeth Palace, the home of the

Archbishop of Canterbury! The young visionaries were to learn wisdom, but for all the furor, we felt Heaven smiling. The cloud of witnesses sharing raised eyebrows maybe, but London had been impacted and the City definitely knew that God's television channel was broadcasting. And some of the buses were still circling Trafalgar Square and Westminster with "GOD" emblazoned on them, until the end of January!

Early 1998 found us miraculously resettled in a purpose-built studio complex that the Lord had found for us through an amazing deal with the Gateshead Council in the North East of England. And so it was that during this period, the Lord started to stretch our imaginations with the most incredible vision. Two credible and trusted prophetic voices had started to talk about the fact that what we were doing, up until then, had been nothing but a pinprick compared to what the Lord had for us in the future – that we would birth a superhighway of anointing through television that would eventually expand and stretch across the globe.

And so it was that the Lord started to speak to us about a multi-channel television platform for the Body of Christ that would be separated from the world, without the sexual innuendo and increasingly violent images that were broadcast across secular television screens each day. That as He was starting to raise up His Body into holiness, He would have them separated from the worldliness of secular television so that every Christian home could have the opportunity to watch television that was "Safe viewing in a secular world."

This led us to investigate satellite systems across Europe and we eventually felt the Holy Spirit leading us to Sirius, one of General Electric's satellite platforms. In faith we signed with them. But what was to follow was one of the most frustrating years of our lives.

It is very common for young visionaries to pre-empt the timing of the plan of God and so it was for us in 1998. The plan of God for a multi-channel platform was right and correct but the timing proved to be premature.

Also, by this time, we had started growing at a rapid rate and had doubled our staff. We had taken on anyone who was skilled and able because we were so desperate for help. And as God always did, there was no getting away from it, He was still holding us on a tight reign. The tool He normally used to get our attention was finance, or rather the lack of it. So for the majority of 1998 we pushed and we strived to get the multi-channel underway instead of concentrating on the field in front of us. (At this time, don't forget, we were still only broadcasting for seven hours a day.)

Yes, Joseph had gone to the cupboard, unrolled the rather dusty multi-colored coat and was now presuming to go from Australasia to Asia, from Africa to America and beyond! Until the creditors weren't just knocking on the door, they were banging on the gates VERY loudly.

With loud reluctant visionary sighs, the coat (and the world domination) was shelved and now we faced ANOTHER terrifying Christmas, which meant we didn't have the faintest hope of survival. How would our staff be paid? Nothing was moving. The vision was stagnant. Every promise's fulfillment seemed to be light years away. We had sent out over fifty letters of appeal to the ministries on our platform. (We even sealed them with silver wax!) We piled them up and laid hands on the mound, before sending them to the four corners of the earth.

No response. Still no help. Finally we sent out a video letter. In November we held our first Partners' Meeting in Birmingham but in the natural it still looked as though we would hardly survive the month.

And so we were in God's great refining process again, on the Potter's wheel. Actually we were in the furnace with the glass door locked firmly ... being baked. And no amount of shouting or screaming for help from the inside was any use.

Now and then there would be a vague sense of our wonderful omnipotent Father's presence as He leant down to check on His fledglings, but all we felt was the heat being turned up! (Ah, so I joke but we know that the Father has such love and tender mercies for all His apostolic visionaries who are called in this end time to do His will upon the earth.)

By January, our final humbling came as the day for our London Partners' Meeting dawned with the worst fog the city had experienced for years. Although all 1,200 seats had been reserved by our viewers weeks in advance, on the actual night, only about 400 viewers actually arrived and our pride and flesh were suffering the fact that we knew our enemies were gloating. More crucifixion. Unfortunately as in Jesus' day, the devil tries to ensure that the crucifixions are very public. However, the Father in His omnipotence knows that sometimes, although cruel on our flesh, it is actually His Sovereign Plan that is being outworked.

I have to add that the London Partners' evening, although poorly attended, not only raised a staggering 1.2 million pounds ($2 million) from our viewers, but that the night itself was saturated with the presence and the favor of God. It was on that same evening we publicly gave the ministry back to God and gave up any ambition of twenty-four hours or the multi-channel. And so we pruned radically, slashed our overheads, let some staff go and THEN cut back our airtime from seven to six hours. Finally we were fully prepared to do HIS bidding and were ready to risk the derision of our enemies. (Could any good thing come out of Nazareth?)

We understood that although we were in television, we could not be seduced by it. We were God's ministry. Gradually the heat started to abate and lo and behold, one morning we pushed the furnace door and it flung open. About to take place was one of the most incredible miracles in our whole ministry – through an incredible couple. Our very precious friends called Albert and Pauline Dicken.

Albert and Pauline were the owners of the very successful North Eastern England DIY Store called "DICKENS." We had met Albert and Pauline at a Benny Hinn Crusade in 1996, and had struck up a great rapport with them. We discovered that we shared a common passion as they *already* had a burning desire to see Christian television in Great Britain and Europe. The reason being – wait for this!

Albert and Pauline had bought a small summer home in Florida some years before and regularly watched *Claude Bowers* television Channel on their television! God had known that a Yorkshire couple would watch the VERY channel who had given us the seed money for GOD TV and that our paths were to cross some years later! God had birthed the desire to see Christian television in the United Kingdom strongly in their heart. By the time we had met together at the crusade in London, we had already launched the Channel a year earlier and were already in the process of moving to Sunderland! (a few miles from where the Dickens lived).

So, it was the very definite beginnings of a divine connection that was to span many years.

Let me elaborate. I need to emphasize here to explain the huge significance of the miracle that was about to occur. AT THAT STAGE, Albert and Pauline, although owning Dickens had absolutely NO SPARE CASH to give to the Channel. EVERYTHING they owned was completely locked up in their DIY business.

Albert grew very close to us over the next few years, standing with us through very many challenges with his own special brand of canny solid Northern wisdom that we learned to treasure. He became a trustee in the very early years, and so VERY many board meetings were spent with Albert and ourselves deliberating over a million ways to try to find money to sustain the Channel. *Especially* at this crucial time where the Channel was in the most dire financial state we had ever been in. We had no way of raising funds. The only thing we knew to do was to all cry out to the Lord for help like the Psalmist King David, before us.

Then THE MIRACLE happened – A sovereign move straight from the very hand of God.

In 1999 – Dickens, although an exceptionally well run prestigious family business, had itself been going through challenging times, as many in the North East were, and business was not quite as flourishing as it had been in earlier years.

That is what makes the hand of God ahead even *more* supernatural.

Suddenly, in the middle of GOD TV's most dire financial time, Albert and Pauline received an out of the blue offer from the largest most affluent British DIY Giant to buy out the *entire family business*. God had hooked the Retail Giant in by their nose because of the positioning of the "Dickens" land which was situated in prime position next to one of the major highways – such an excellent location.

Because of this UK Retail giant's desire to own the land, they put forward an unprecedented deal and offered Albert and Pauline an unprecedented and substantial amount of money.

The deal went through so swiftly, with few hindrances, and *suddenly* Albert Dicken, trusty member of our board who had had no ready cash to gift into the ministry and had been through hell and back with us – was now a *millionaire!* We all nearly fell backwards!

Albert and Pauline had established a Charitable Trust in 1977 with objectives to see the Kingdom of God extended. This was an ideal place to deposit most of the money. Within weeks they had gifted over FOUR million pounds ($7 million) from the trust to the struggling

155

GOD TV. This move of God was one of the most sovereign things that Rory and I had ever experienced in our whole eleven years at GOD TV.

Through the years, the Dicken's trust has continued on occasion to assist GOD TV. They have the most wonderful generous, servant hearts. They have stuck with GOD TV through the wildest storms and we can only give God the glory for these two incredible people – servants of the Most High. Albert still stands with us passionately looking for other sources of revenue (as you will know well if you've watched him on Missions week! If you have any questions concerning donating to GOD TV – he'd LOVE to answer them!). Albert flies with Rory on occasion to meet with potential donors.

We cannot thank them both enough for their love, commitment and unfailing dedication to the work of GOD TV. Only when Albert and Pauline stand before the Lord in the Courts of Heaven will they truly see the incredible impact of their joyful generous giving. We love and are so grateful to them for that – but we loved them long before any of it even existed – they are dear, dear friends.

Without people like these, the Gospel would have taken far longer to be preached. Time is so short. We honor them and all those who sow so generously into GOD TV. Always.

The following four months saw the operational infrastructure well underway – the library management systems were installed, transmission suites were built, satellite uplinks installed, contracts signed with the Sirius satellite providers and then there came another amazing breakthrough – we signed a contract enabling the GOD Channel to broadcast for twenty-four hours a day on the new Sky Digital Platform.

On 1 October, 1999, our fourth birthday, we launched the first twenty-four-hour Christian signal to ever broadcast daily in Britain on the Sky Digital Platform. Two weeks later, we beamed four twenty-four-hour streams up twenty-two thousand kilometers to the Sirius satellite and righteousness started to rain down across Europe and the Middle East.

But we were now in a complete state of flux! Not only had we just grown from a six-hour daily service to a brand new daily twenty-four-hour television service, but we were also running a multi-channel. Next to Sky Digital and On Digital we were Britain's third multi-channel!

We were still as usual desperately understaffed (we employed over one hundred people but needed another hundred at least). It was all we could do to keep the television signals on air each day, let alone to put all our exhausted and now totally stretched Gideon's army to work to marshal new viewing partners as well! But we had to because this was to be God's new paradigm. So in the first few weeks of a very difficult birth, the hastily set up marketing department managed to scrape together a rather make-shift piece of information, which we sent out to any poor unsuspecting viewer who had in the past made contact with us.

As make-shift as the leaflet had been, the response we received was so overwhelming in the first launch weeks, that it almost brought the entire Channel to a standstill. We had made a commitment to launch by giving boxes away, like Sky Digital and On Digital, to make it easier for our viewers to switch on but each shipment of five thousand boxes cost half a million pounds! ($800,000).

Meanwhile the Channel's phone lines were coming to a standstill. There was absolutely no way imaginable that we could cope with the calls. Calls were quite literally going EVERYWHERE, to transmission, finance, engineering, production, to anyone of our staff who would by this time dare to pick up the phone. We immediately decided that there was no option but to outsource it. Gradually the frenzy seemed to subside, only NOW we had the DISH problem.

The problem was very simple. Because we were once again pioneering, and our satellite footprint covered not only the whole of the UK, but also stretched over Russia, North Africa and to Lebanon and Israel, we couldn't use a small dish like Sky Digital but started off by using what one of our staff affectionately called "a wok." But more of a problem was that the installers who were only used to locating Sky Digital's satellite coordinates in the sky, were almost at a complete loss when it came to locating the Sirius satellite.

The next horror that reared its ugly head was that after our patient, long-suffering subscribers had got past the ever engaged phone lines and the installer nightmare they came up against the "BRACKET" saga ... We had consulted long and hard with the very top end of industry expertise and the bolts chosen, we were promised, were the best and only route to go. Hmmm. No sooner were the first thousands of dishes installed, our phone lines became jam-packed again, ringing off the hook day and night because each time the howling October and November winds blew across Britain, the dishes moved. The reason was that the brackets had been put in wrongly by the installers. This did not prove to be a quick fix.

As many of our viewers stretched across the British Isles, as soon as we sorted out Humberside, Scotland started to blow, then Ireland and so on. Every time Britain experienced bad winds, we held our breaths. We became experts on weather patterns, but unfortunately the bracket problem continued for some time. Some viewers lost their cool and more than one, we have to admit, actually swore down the phone at our client service staff. But others were wonderfully long-suffering and understood the pioneering challenges. One dear partner was reduced to having a moving satellite dish waving precariously on a pole at the back of his house as it was the only way he could get a reasonable signal!

Gradually, things started to calm down and the teething

problems, one by one, started to be ironed out. But then we had the programing issue . . .

We were faced with a mammoth task. We were now running a huge monster called "Television" that consumed programing minute by minute, twenty-four hours a day, every day, every week, all year round and we were originating not just ONE twenty-four-hour channel, the GOD Channel – but we launched a second twenty-four-hour GOD Channel, then known as the Revival Channel.

The demand of the two channels for programing was voracious. We were faced with two immediate hurdles, the first being our miniscule (compared to secular broadcasters) Acquisitions and Programing Budget which had been eaten up almost in the first three months of launching the multi-channel. (BSkyB's program budget in 1999 was 790 million pounds! – $1.4 million.)

Our second challenge was the fact that Christian Television in America had never had programing as its priority and therefore over the forty years since its inception, had barely produced any programs at all, just its flagship vision sharing programs and quite literally a handful of kids and youth material. This meant that after five years of executing, what our programing department affectionately called "scouring the whole earth searching for Christian programs," we could almost count the Christian productions available for broadcast on two hands.

We immediately acquired the European rights to *Bibleman*, *Testament*, *Storykeepers*, *Present Time*, *McGee and Me*, most of the Christian film packages that existed and everything else that was affordable and of a reasonable broadcast standard. The first problem was that by Easter the network had consumed nearly every suitable available Christian program that we knew of and couldn't discover much more to acquire. The second problem was that almost everything was American as hardly anyone else in the entire world produced anything vaguely Christian that was of a high enough standard for television broadcast!

By this time our operational costs had escalated to horrifying amounts and we had nothing left for original production at the studios. But we had no option, we had to make productions. So late 1999 saw the unique concept of *Dream on TV* broadcast at 10.00 p.m., Tuesday to Thursday which broadcast a radio format in the radio studio onto TV. *In Depth* grabbed every unsuspecting preacher, teacher and guest who happened to wend their unsuspecting way up to Gateshead to visit and boy, did we get as many programs out of them in a day, keeping our costs as low as possible. I think the record was when we filmed sixteen programs of *In Depth* in two days. (Although Bill Wilson came a close second when we captured him on his way from New York with thirty-two five-minute programs in a day!)

Then came *Dream Kids, DK Extreme*, our two-hour Sunday afternoon wrap-around. In fact towards the end of the year 2000 we had produced over fifty hours of children's programing; 200 hours of Youth Programing, including *Dream on TV*; *Entertainment News*; *Scene Dock* and *CMTV*; and 160 hours of interviews including *Behind the Screens, In Depth* and *Walk Right In*. We also filmed a staggering 400 hours of programing from Outside Broadcast Units including filming with the Assemblies of God; Spring Harvest and Easter People; together with live broadcasts from Sweden, Latvia, Russia and Germany and even covering two of Morning Star's Conferences in America; plus linking live to T. D. Jakes' *Woman Thou Art Loosed* Conferences in Atlanta; Kenneth Copeland in Bournemouth; and Rodney Howard-Browne's New York Crusade held in Madison Square Gardens.

By the end of the year, we felt God was saying we needed to communicate with our viewers through a flagship program. This was to incorporate inserts showing different aspects of the vision in a format that was more sophisticated than the long-suffering *Good Morning Europe* and *Behind the Screens* programs.

And because for five years we had really put production value into the GOD Channel and our premier programs, our own flagship program was looking extremely the worse for wear and bore absolutely no resemblance to what we saw in our minds. Now, at last, we had an opportunity to upgrade our own program, which would re-launch on Sunday 3rd December with a totally new look. And now to the real behind the screens that night! Forty-eight hours before our first *Sunday Night Live*, the set was still being erected and the lighting was only finished fifteen minutes before we were going live on air! That left us just ten minutes to rehearse. So of course we only rehearsed our first link before the countdown sounded. Just to add to the drama, as we went live, my earpiece quite literally FLEW out of my ear and I got the giggles as we started to read the menu. The worst thing about when you lose it, is that you are LIVE. Somehow I managed to stop laughing by the time the menu was off and it was back to Rory and me.

Everything went smoothly until, with one minute to go, Rory and I got rather too enthusiastic and insisted on taking another call.

The *Behind the Screens* situation was not as calm as the "on screen." The urgent turning into VERY urgent sounds of our director counting down in our ear while our producer, across the way from us, was making VERY obvious "Wrap up" signs from the floor while our second caller was unwittingly conducting a discourse on the weather in France. This had me and Rory flummoxed as to how to end the twenty-second conversation without abruptly cutting off our poor viewer. We eventually came out in time just to run our end credits.

Not as bad, may I add, as our LIVE from Uppsala debut in the Dream Radio Studios. We thought we had been playing out a transmission from Uppsala, but found out at the end of the evening from Bo, our correspondent there that night, they had been watching us ALL off air!

They had sat aghast at the church in Sweden for SIX whole minutes while the cameras were filming all of us in the studio as we were unaware we were being filmed. THAT must have been interesting!

I have to admit that I never quite worked up the courage to watch that *faux pas* but I had hysterics at what the viewers must have thought ... There we were with no sound, just pictures, with Rory waving his credit card high in the air. What had people thought!!! I had visions of the skeptics concluding that we were so money and prosperity-orientated, we must have been discussing donations from viewers or some money raising strategy! Never fear, dearest viewers! It was nothing more macabre than choosing between pizza and Kentucky Fried Chicken with Rory offering up his credit card to our trusty cameraman, Mick, to buy dinner for everyone in the studio!

What an unintentional *Behind the Screens* that was!

Oh, there are so many stories to tell. THERE ARE SO MANY MIRACLES THAT OUR FATHER HAS DONE FOR US but we want you to know that we love and appreciate you so very much – your prayers, your commitment to this ministry, your support, and above all your unfailing enthusiasm and love for us and our wonderful apostolic team.

It is only through the partnership of our viewers that we can fulfill God's awesome call to take the Gospel to the lost through television. We are totally dependent on God moving on the hearts and minds of His people to support us, knowing that every partner in every Christian household in every town and city across the nations enables us to go to the next level to fulfill the Father's plan for a NEW BREED of Christian television.

The apostolic breakthrough anointing of GOD TV had broken

through the airwaves, clearing the way in later years for multitudes of Christian channels from all across the world to broadcast across the airwaves of Great Britain.

A deathblow to the Prince of the Power of the Airwaves over Great Britain. We now had large studios in Newcastle, a transmission center and an uplink of our own and were broadcasting *one channel* twenty-four hours a day to Britain and Europe, producing thousands of hours of original programing a year. We were also broadcasting across the nations of Europe. *Then* God spoke a strong directional word that would literally change the direction of the future of GOD TV. We had always known as visionaries that GOD TV's destiny was Jerusalem but as Rory was praying the Lord said:

"Move the broadcast Headquarters to Jerusalem."

Like Abraham, the Lord had said "GO!"

And so, in obedience, as visionaries – we obeyed.

The sovereign plan of Almighty God for GOD TV was about to open up before us in an incredible and unprecedented manner.

CHAPTER EIGHTEEN

THE NATIONS – BROADCASTING FROM JERUSALEM TO THE UTTERMOST PARTS OF THE EARTH

ESTABLISHING THE MINISTRY of GOD TV has been a road filled with high risk, great leaps of faith, presumption, repentance, heart-breaking betrayals, perseverance, ministerial politics, exhilaration and much suffering. The testings have been overwhelming, for the Kingdom of God comes by violence and the violent take it by force. The temptations have been many, on every level, yet somehow even in those tempestuous times, when the satanic forces were howling, the voice that spoke the world into existence whispered, "Hold on," and the everlasting arms held us firmly until the raging storms subsided.

Surely this road is not for the fainthearted, and yet in our own strength we would have failed, for without Him we are nothing and all attempts by our own hand are doomed to failure. And so as the years have gone by, we have finally started to understand that in our own natural selves, we had nothing to give Him, that we are completely dependent on His grace and on His great mercies.

Our ambitions and any gifting or talents entrusted to us, the Father has no need of. He can do it all, without us, at any time but in His great compassion and by His sovereign hand, He has, from the foundations of the earth, chosen to use us to do this work.

And so, very slowly, we started to glimpse His long-term divine purposes for GOD TV. What had begun as another Christian television channel, in the same mold as other American pioneers, we perceived He was now developing into a different tool for a brand new purpose. We were to be a battering-ram in the Spirit that would war with the devil in the high places of the earth – the air-waves – to preach the Gospel to the lost, standing back to back with the leading secular channels, having an excellence of programing and presentation that would compete with them, but be broadcasting a message that was roaring with Holy Ghost power and conviction as it broadcast into people's living rooms all across the globe.

We were to become God's voice through the nations, to bring down to earth the Father's own program schedule from the throne room and herald in new voices and become a platform for fresh anointings. God's prophetic cry would be heard across the airwaves. His prophetic teachers would teach the new wine. GOD TV would cry out into the spirit realm, "Thus saith the Lord." The destiny of the Church of Jesus Christ would start to change and be repositioned across Europe, Asia, Africa, Australia and the Middle East and eventually to the Americas and the uttermost ends of the earth.

For as GOD TV entered into the third millennium, surely this was a ministry ordained by the Father, as one of His tools to usher in His end-time move generationally across the earth. Television, the very tool used by Satan to control and pervert the minds and hearts of this last generation, would be used by the Father to deal the devil his death blow and to usher in the end-time move of His Spirit, presenting Him with a Bride that was to be without spot, wrinkle or blemish and to bring Him souls, souls, souls, multitudes of souls that had been blinded by humanism and shackled by the fetters of unbelief.

And so, although moving our broadcast center from Newcastle to Israel would mean a radical shift in our thinking and an incredible upheaval in logistics, we knew that GOD had spoken. So in obedience, our teams working around the clock, we moved our entire transmission facility from Newcastle, England to just outside Jerusalem. The incredible miracle today, dear friends, is that we have just completed our new broadcast center in Jerusalem at the foot of MOUNT ZION. And today as I write – we beam out **NINE** *different channels – GOD CHANNEL, GOD UK, GOD AFRICA, GOD ASIA, GOD MIDDLE EAST, GOD AUSTRALASIA, GOD SCANDANAVIA, THE INTERNET FEED and now also GOD USA* broadcasting the Word of Almighty God from Mount Zion in Jerusalem into over 200 nations across the globe to over 438 million viewers – over 122 million television households.

But at that stage of the vision, it was 2001 and we were still only broadcasting on one twenty-four-hour channel to the United Kingdom and to parts of Europe! We had absolutely NO idea of the immense global growth that would occur in the future. It took all our energy and faith to just try to survive the DAY!!

So it took an incredible leap of faith, not only for us as visionaries but for our amazing GOD TV team who mobilized behind us, but we all began to sense in a very powerful way that this was prophecy being fulfilled before our very eyes.

> "... *Come and let us go up to the mountain of the* LORD
> *And to the and to house of the God of Jacob* ...
> *For from Zion will go forth the law,*
> *Even the Word of the* LORD *from Jerusalem.*"

(Micah 4:2 NASB)

166

We felt that this was the most significant announcement that GOD TV had made since the birth of the Christian Channel. Never before has man had the ability to span the globe with the Gospel. Never before has God released His Word and His truth as He is doing in these last days. And Jerusalem is the center of it all.

Skeptics may ask, "Who in their right mind would move to Israel, with the volatile political climate of the Middle East?" But Jerusalem is where our Lord Jesus walked, where He died and where He rose again. Jerusalem is where He ascended into Heaven, and most significantly, where He will return.

The GOD Channel is His Channel and we both felt strongly along with our key team that Jerusalem was the place where we needed our broadcast headquarters to be. This single act of obedience was to open up unimaginable distribution possibilities for the ministry of GOD TV, immediately facilitating the inclusion of the GOD Channel on a number of new satellite positions. By simply moving our satellite uplink to Jerusalem, we now found out that we would now be able to take advantage of a number of unique satellite configurations, which would position us to impact the world with the Gospel of Jesus Christ. We had had no inkling of the possibilities! God's Word would beam up from Jerusalem to touch the whole world with His love and compassion and the Gospel of His Son.

Our wonderful British viewers had caught the excitement of GOD TV's vision and the e-mails and letters of encouragement from our partners literally flooded in, with comments ranging from "I nearly fell off the couch when I heard the news..." to a deep acknowledgment of the profound significance of the move.

Pastor Matthew Ashimolowo of Kingsway International Christian Church (KICC) in London, was a particular blessing. He said that the move was not only spiritually significant, but also strategic and smart. "We appreciate the way God has used you," he said. "Thank you for being faithful to the vision, you have been pioneers in the

realm of Christian media in Europe and as you step into new
territories, we trust the Lord will continue to bless your work. You
should not be in this alone, we stand with you shoulder to shoulder,
understanding the fact that we are touching the world before our
Savior's return."

Rory and I were also given confirmation from the Word through
Isaiah 54:2–3:

> *"Enlarge the place of your tent;*
> *Stretch out the curtains of your dwellings, spare not;*
> *Lengthen your cords*
> *And strengthen your pegs.*
> *For you will spread abroad to the right and to the left.*
> *And your descendants will possess nations..."*
>
> (NASB)

And so, Rory and I, and our Head of Distribution, met with a satellite
communications company to sign a deal which would allow GOD TV
to relocate our two channels to Jerusalem and from there to broadcast God's prophetic end-time agenda to "the uttermost parts of the
earth."

Or course, this did not come without a major annual financial
commitment – in fact an increased budget shortfall of three and a
half million pounds ($6 million), but so inspired were our partners in
the United Kingdom and Europe, that the video letter announcing
the move raised over one million pounds, with the balance to follow
in our first Missions Week on air appeal.

We knew that God was calling us to serve as a prophetic voice to
the nations and that Jerusalem was a key to our fulfilling His call.
Jerusalem is at the heart of God's plan for man and a strategic focal
point in world events. Above all, now it is the center for the twenty-
four-hour broadcast of God's Word from the heart of the City of

David. Our GOD TV broadcast team in Israel do an amazing job and now the entire ministry of GOD TV serves as a prophetic media tool in God's hands and help the Body of Christ to grow in its understanding of God's prophetic agenda for Israel.

Jerusalem is the real "Ground Zero."

I remember vividly the early days of my first visits to Israel. I would be completely baffled because I knew that so many, many people got so blessed when they visited there. But that wasn't true for me; from the moment that I set foot on the land some years ago, I felt the worlds violently colliding in the spirit realm around us. It was a violent tinderbox in the spirit realm and I experienced tremendous warfare and resistance each time I set foot on the ground of Israel.

But over these past few years, I have sensed a strong definable shift in the spirit where the havoc in the spirit realm has lessened. In this past season when we go to Israel, even when politically it is like a tinderbox, in the spirit realm, I can tangibly sense the protection and the unseen fortress of the Lord.

I believe the significant change is thanks to the thousands and thousands of faithful intercessors both inside and outside Israel who pray fervently for the peace of Jerusalem and for God's Kingdom to come in Israel and the Middle East. This is a huge cornerstone of GOD TV's mandate for the Middle East – that GOD TV would be a prophetic voice to the Middle Eastern region, that we would mobilize intercessors and prayer warriors all across the nations to pray and stand with our Arab and Jewish brothers and sisters in Christ both in Israel and the Middle East.

This end-time call from God for GOD TV in this area has been the cause of much spiritual warfare and opposition against us, not only in the spirit realm but in the natural. But we have to be obedient to God.

It is a place that everyone is fighting over, but so few understand. Jerusalem is truly God's city, a place that He has chosen, a place to which the Lord Jesus will return to collect His Body, the Glorious Church. Even as I write, Israel and Lebanon are at war and we have had the privilege of broadcasting from Jerusalem a call to Prayer, to mobilize our viewers in these crucial end-time days to pray for the peace and the destiny of Jerusalem, of Israel and of the Middle East.

But back to the first unprepossessing days in 2002, when we set up our broadcast center to transmit one GOD TV channel with our tiny team in Israel. In a matter of months, the world literally began to open up as God Himself sovereignly began to open great doors of utterance for GOD TV.

In April 2002 we received a delegation from India who arrived at Angel House in Newcastle, England, led by Dr Paul Dhinakharan from Chennai. His father, such a precious father in Christ and God's Prophet – Brother DGS Dhinakharan, had received a strong word from the Lord that a significant part of GOD TV's destiny was to broadcast into India.

Our attention was arrested that day. These are such wonderful Indian brothers with such precious spirits and we knew that the Lord was speaking through them. Well, sitting around the table with them was a gentleman they had brought with them called Thomas Robinson. Thomas had had a top position with ESPN and MTV and then got saved. He had a burning passion to see the Gospel proclaimed through the media. He was part of the delegation and working with the Dhinakharan's ministry as a media consultant. Both Rory and I had a strong impression that Thomas was meant to work for GOD TV and head up the region of India. We left it in the Lord's hands.

By a matter of divine circumstance, Thomas Robinson started as Regional Director of Asia and what an incredible blessing he has been. He has pioneered GOD TV's outreach throughout Asia facing multiple challenges on every front daily. On 31 May 2002, our first historic broadcast beamed into five million Indian homes. By the end of the first year distribution had grown to ten million homes! Today, we broadcast to over THIRTY million cable homes across the great nation of India.

When Pastor Benny Hinn went out to India to conduct his crusade – Rory was standing on the platform with him when he asked who watched GOD TV. The miracle is that in those crowds of millions, hundreds of thousands of hands went up and the hands kept going and going ... and going!

Oh how we love India and the Indian people. And not only India is being reached by the Gospel through GOD TV but also the surrounding areas of South East Asia. Thirty five cable operators in Nepal carry GOD TV including the capital Katmandu – GOD TV also broadcasts into Afghanistan, Burma, Cambodia, Hong Kong, China, Fiji, India, Indonesia, Korea, Kazakhstan, Laos, Malaysia, Mongolia, Nepal, Pakistan, Sri Lanka, Tajikistan, Thailand, Turkmenistan and Uzbekistan and Vietnam. Our Asian GOD TV team do the most phenomenal job, led by Thomas Robinson, as do all our Regional Directors across the world and their teams in the UK, Scandinavian, German, African and American offices. We honor them and their faithful, committed teams tremendously.

Our very first broadcasts into the continent of Africa from Cape Town to Cairo on the PAS-7 and THAICOM satellites were also transmitted on 31 May 2002. Excited phone calls and emails from all across Africa flooded into GOD TV as viewers started connecting to the GOD Channel Africa feed via satellite, from Libya to Zimbabwe and South Africa where GOD TV has its African office in Cape Town. We have passionately taken up Reinhard Bonnke's battle cry ... "From Cape Town to Cairo, Africa shall be saved." South Africa's response to GOD TV was overwhelming, and was quickly followed by Zimbabwe and the continent of Africa.

We have also been deeply touched by the heartfelt responses from across Libya and Ethiopia, where underground believers are using the broadcasts as their church and spiritual food. There is even a television in the airport in Kenya transmitting a twenty-four-hour feed! But we knew that to truly reach Africa, we needed to get our broadcasts into the villages, so GOD TV developed a strategy to build ten transmitters in five different countries within the next season, from Ghana to Uganda, Kenya, Namibia and Lesotho. Three of these transmitters are already operational in Kenya, in Eldoret, Timboroa and Matchakos (Nairobi) reaching a further fifteen million African viewers.

Directly after our Jerusalem launch, GOD TV also began broadcasting to a potential eighteen million Ugandans six hours each morning through a partnership with Uganda Television. Now GOD TV is looking to build its own transmitter in this revival hotspot, covering the whole nation twenty-four/seven.

Africa continues to expand rapidly every day and today the GOD TV signal broadcasts to Angola, Botswana, Burkina Faso, Cameroon, Central African Republic, Democratic Republic of Congo (Zaire), Ethiopia, Gabon, Ghana, Ivory Coast, Kenya, Lesotho, Libya, Malawi, Morocco, Mozambique, Namibia, Nigeria, Rwanda, Sierra Leone, Somalia, South Africa, Sudan, Swaziland, Tanzania and Togo.

At the end of 2002, GOD TV's broadcasts were on seven satellites covering four-fifths of the globe and broadcasting to 199 countries.

But despite the world opening up to us, since our early days of struggle the United States of America had called to us like a homing beacon. We had sensed strongly that God had a specific vital role that lay ahead that He had destined GOD TV for in America. We had thought we would launch into America years ago – and America had been a vital part of our launch. God had connected GOD TV and America even from its inception in London, England. And had used both Benny Hinn and Claude Bowers and his board of Superchannel in our very early incredibly challenging prelaunch days to launch into the United Kingdom and Europe.

And so it was that after we had launched in Britain and moved to Jerusalem, we started to hear the Lord's whisper "America ... America..."

And we said, "But Father, America is saturated with Christian television." And the Lord said "You don't understand – I want to do a new thing in the airwaves and GOD TV is an integral part of it – Be obedient."

We knew that the Lord had spoken. And so we packed up our house in England and within weeks we were on our way to the United States of America.

The long and arduous journey ahead had begun.

CHAPTER NINETEEN

JOURNEY TO THE NEW WORLD

WELL, AS TRUSTY PIONEERS like Abraham thousands of years before us when he was called to a nation he did not know, we were going by faith to the United States of America.

We packed up enough clothes and belongings that would last us the first six months of our stay in the New World into one *mammoth* suitcase. We had decided that we would sail to the New World and use it as a short holiday on the way after our grueling visionary schedules of the past few years and try to rest.

So we procured ourselves transatlantic "bucket" tickets at out of season rates. Yes! It was WINTER. Were we crazy? – YES! Of course we were! But brave missionary pioneers often don't KNOW what's ahead – (that's why they can seem brave!) because if we could have seen the whole picture – we may not have ever left Southampton docks! But leave them we did.

It was a cold British winter's day on 16 December 2002 – as the new "Plymouth Brethren-Alec family" waved goodbye to England

and sailed away from Southampton, the shores of Great Britain. And like those great Pilgrim pioneers before us, we headed directly toward the East Coast of America – the City of New York. Well – the great journey had begun! We were ALL crammed into one cabin and we *suddenly* realized why the tickets were so much cheaper.

Sailing in mid-December was not exactly a summer experience of reclining on deck chairs and swimming in the several pools on deck.

It was not only freezing and raining, so the pools were closed, but far more chilling was the fact that the cheaper tickets meant in plain language – *"You may encounter some hair-raising storms along the way that could make even the most trusty Christian pioneers extremely seasick!"* And indeed – we DID!

The height of the waves at times was unimaginable. The ship rocked often incessantly from side to side. I mean from SIDE to SIDE! What was worse, was that every time the ship rocked, Christian and Samantha's camp beds flew violently across the cabin in a heap directly towards us.

In the midst of THAT scenario, *every* time we sat down at the dinner table, like clockwork, our poor languishing eight-year-old son, Christian, would turn a pale tinge of green and then would run urgently out through the wooden doors.

Finally, much to our relief – and possibly the entire passenger list, our ship docked in New York Harbor on 21 December.

The Alec family had landed in the New World – the land of Christian television opportunity. Our pioneering bravado already slightly jaded, we now discovered that we had just landed in one of the *largest* snowstorms of the century that the city of New York had ever seen. We drove through Manhattan passing the site of 9/11 on the way to the hotel.

It was CHRISTMAS week and for some reason which we still can't place today (in retrospect it may have been fuelled by movie images of New York at Christmas from *Home Alone*!), we were SURE that New York at Christmas would be an amazing experience. Unforgettable. It was for the first two days . . .

Well, we rushed out to "Macys" because that was the only place as English visitors we knew where to shop and our twelve-year-old daughter somehow proceeded to spill a huge raspberry drink all over her clothes which left large purple stains and sent us scurrying up and down escalators looking for replacements. We didn't know a solitary soul!

But December 25 arrived and on opening the curtains we discovered in bewilderment that in one day nearly EVERYONE had fled New York. Hardly a soul could be seen on the streets.

It was CHRISTMAS and NEW YORK seemed DESERTED. How strange, we thought!

Where were the Hollywood movie images of thronging streets and festivities??

After trawling the streets of New York for open restaurants, we eventually found a solitary restaurant around the corner that was actually open on Christmas Day. I remember phoning my parents in Dorset in England, feeling slightly desolate inside. But of course – we, the Alec family were the dread breakthrough Pilgrim pioneers. And as we had left with many voices telling us, "Why America – are you crazy?", we felt we couldn't so readily admit to defeat. So with a trembling voice, I put best foot forward to the parents.

"How is New York?" asked my mother in a suspicious tone.

"Oh WONDERFUL Mum – just wonderful . . ." I said gaily, picking at my Christmas dinner. "Couldn't be better!"

"Are you *sure* you're alright?" asked my compassionate but extremely discerning Father.

"Yes . . . Yes – we're great . . . " My voice trailed off thinking of the Christmas tree at their house with all the presents surrounding it and the turkey that would no doubt be on the dining-room table with all the trimmings, circled by the family, cousins and friends.

And so we finished our desultory Christmas Pilgrim's dinner and the morning after Boxing Day began the second stage of our Pilgrim's Progress – to Charlotte, North Carolina to our friends at Morningstar.

Well – the kindness and compassion of Rick and Julie Joyner is legendary! The men and women of Morningstar and at Moravian Falls were so *very* kind and hospitable. The first week Rick arranged a get together at which our friend Leonard Jones, who has always loved GOD TV with a passion, had a strong word for us. He told us that our experience in America would be different from what we had imagined – and would take MUCH longer, but that God's purpose WOULD happen. Oh Leonard – what a welcome! Our hearts were sinking. But – you were so right!

We stayed in the "Box House" at Moravian Falls, courtesy of Rick, for several months. We managed to get some bedroom furniture, but never quite got to filling the lounge. We entered a difficult season, that looking back now, we are so blessed that we were able to go through it.

Once again it was a stripping, humbling process. With events ahead, we are so very, very glad that we experienced it. Suddenly Rory and I found ourselves in America where GOD TV was completely UNKNOWN!!! God had done such an incredible miracle in our midst – but the only Christian television that was known here was TBN and Daystar and the local Christian stations.

It was a tremendous personal growth experience.

It was a bit like Billy Graham going to a land where they had never heard of his ministry and had absolutely no knowledge of the influence or mission and of his call. And leaving *all his staff behind*.

There were a few hardy souls of great encouragement who had watched GOD TV on the internet and had "got it" – but the majority in the USA – although extremely courteous and polite, gave that semi-glazed look when we spoke about a new move in the airwaves. With sinking hearts, we knew that the huge challenge that faced us both as visionaries was that until GOD TV actually LAUNCHED into the USA – there were not very many people who would stand with us and truly understand the mandate and the call from the Father upon GOD TV. *Because they had NEVER "SEEN" GOD TV!*

We believed with ALL our hearts that God had called GOD TV to broadcast a new apostolic prophetic evangelistic schedule into living rooms all across America, that there was a schedule in Heaven specifically created by the Lord that would bring his new streams together to combine with that which had gone before to birth a prophetic television network that would cry out across America – "THUS SAITH THE LORD!" And it would be one of God's end-time tools for revival in these last days. But of course – Satan – the Prince of the Power of the Air would fight us every step of the way – doing all in his power to keep GOD TV out of America.

The battles began in earnest. They were different battles from our early struggles in Great Britain – yet much was the same. It WAS INCREDIBLE.

We had faced the fiercest opposition in Great Britain when we had started to launch GOD TV. Now, nearly nine years later, although firmly established in nearly all major continents of the world, the fight against the launch of GOD TV in America by the powers of darkness was as fierce, maybe even more intense in opposition against us, than when we had first broken through the gates of brass in Great Britain and Europe.

We literally had arrived, it felt like, to start from scratch and pioneer just as we had done all those years before in England. But we knew what God had said.

So with virtually NO team, working from two desks and a phone from the Box House in Moravian Falls, *we started GOD TV in the USA.*

We began to look around Charlotte for premises for GOD TV USA – and had seen several really interesting studio opportunities when the Iraq war broke out.

We rushed up to Washington DC to uplink live to the UK and the world for a live broadcast. And then – completely unexpectedly, God breathed on us, like he did upon Abraham. Suddenly we couldn't leave Washington DC. We simply COULD NOT LEAVE.

It was as though we became hemmed in by the very hand of Almighty God. And the voice of the Lord said – *"I want GOD TV in the Capital City of the United States."*

Nothing had been further from our minds. We were already in negotiation for buildings in Charlotte and had found a disused film set which had enormous potential that we were really excited about. But we knew that God had spoken sovereignly. So on a colleague's recommendation, in faith, we took a trip to Fredericksburg Virginia, 50 miles outside DC.

Well, in a matter of days we had found a house, and a wonderful Christian school for the children. (There was a great miracle connected with this house told later on in these pages.)

Within weeks we had moved, lock, stock and barrel to the East Coast of America – to Virginia.

Swiftly we found premises on M Street, one of Washington DC's main streets – but now we continued to face the greatest challenge of all.

We were IN America. We now had STUDIOS in the very center of Washington DC, four blocks from the White House.

But every single door that we pushed for distribution of GOD TV's signal came to a grinding halt. Every door of utterance in the USA closed to us. Cable operators were waiting for us to launch before they were prepared to take our signal. With the satellite platform Echostar we received so much favor, that the CEO of Echostar himself read our proposal on a plane, but because of certain complex legal obligations to other Christian carriers, we were not allowed to broadcast on their satellites.

Let me say here – there have been some – a handful of Christian television ministries who have been so generous of heart – who have expressed the nature of Jesus to us – and we so love and appreciate their generosity of heart. But several others were skeptical or suspicious of us. We discovered that Christian television is the same all across the world – often it has been infiltrated by a Jezebelic, Babylon spirit which is territorial, political and highly competitive. It has an assignment against many ministries today.

I say that for all of us in Christian television with heartfelt compassion. These are the spirits that we and our team at GOD TV ourselves have had to battle against, in our hearts and in our minds – but dear friends, we want to serve Christ. And if we succumb to the spirits that have often ruled Christian television – how could God use us for a new move? And in this process there is death – each day. Dying to proclaim the Gospel. Dying to selfish ambition. Dying to preserving one's own ministry. Dying to rumors and falsehoods from those who seek our destruction with ambitious intent.

At GOD TV so often we find ourselves,

"... hedged in (pressed) on every side – troubled and oppressed in every way; but not cramped or crushed; we suffer embarrassments and are perplexed and unable to find a way out, but not driven to despair; we are (persecuted and hard driven,) pursued, but not deserted – to stand alone; we are struck down to the ground, but never struck out and destroyed; always carrying about in the body the liability and exposure to the same putting to death that the Lord Jesus suffered, so that the [resurrection-] life of Jesus also may be shown forth by and in our bodies."

(2 Corinthians 4:8–10 AMP)

We will not enter in to political ambition, or divisiveness – or territorialism, which is horrendously hard and challenging when people are vying for your airtime or your distribution opportunities.

But deep in our hearts and souls, the cry of the Holy Spirit rings out –
God is able to keep you – preserve you – lay a table before you. *"Don't
preserve yourselves, beloved. I'll preserve you."*

We started to build our teams.

Our launch date was now set for 2004 – but the gates of the
broadcast industry remained like brass. It was a chicken and egg
situation. "When you launch – we'll look at proposals to put GOD TV
on across America," said the cable operators. But no one was
prepared to take a risk on an unknown channel. They loved our
GOD TV showreels. They would consider putting us on their line-ups
but *ONLY when we launched*.

And all the while, the devil was saying to us "Go Home! Go Back!
Get off these shores!" We could almost hear him hiss. "I will bar the
doors so tightly, you'll never launch!"

And we said, "BUT GOD . . . " clinging to the word we so strongly
believed He had given us.

We were to be tested in the wilderness.

CHAPTER TWENTY
—————————

RAINBOW BRIDGE

Rory FLEW BACK to London to renew our visas. But unfortunately, there were some unforeseen technical hitches and the American Embassy in London required more paperwork, so the visas were deferred.

On Rory's return it was Samantha's thirteenth birthday – and so we decided to celebrate by visiting Niagara Falls. We had a great time. On our first night, outside our hotel room, there was a Bob Dylan concert live and we prayed from our hotel room that the Lord would reveal himself once again to him. Well!

On the way back to Virginia, the following day we gaily handed our British passports to the man at the border which was called "Rainbow Bridge." He took them inside, made a phone call, then walked back over to our car, looking ominously at us.

"That way!" he said rather sternly, pointing towards the immigration offices ahead. With hearts sinking, we parked and were shown to the immigration section, where they rigorously checked Rory's passport.

Rory had had a stamp from the US embassy saying the visas *were* in process. After a long time of consideration, more phone calls and many questions, Rainbow Bridge finally received confirmation that Rory's visa was indeed valid, and was at that exact time in due process. But as the immigration officer flipped through the rest of our passports – he suddenly stopped on Wendy Alec's!

The long finger of the Law beckoned to me.

"Lady!" the burly immigration officer said. His eyes flashed. "You're ten days over on your visa," he growled.

"But our visas were held up in London." I stammered. "They're all in process..."

"We don't *care* about London," he stated. "YOU have violated the visa waiver scheme."

My little beating heart started to sink into the bottom of my boots. I stared at the huge gun in the holster around his waist.

"This is a SERIOUS VIOLATION!" he declared sternly. "THEY" he pointed to Rory, Samantha and Christian. "THEY..." he continued, "can return to Virginia."

"YOU," he glowered darkly at me – the great media pioneer who was trembling from the top of her fingers to the bottom of her boots.

"YOU – can't go back into America!" he stated emphatically. "You've violated your visa."

"But... But..." I echoed feebly. Then, as my daughter tells me, I pulled out my prophetic finger at the immigration officer, my eyes flashing.

"But ALL my *clothes* are in Fredericksburg..." For some strange reason, I must have thought that the stern immigration officer would have compassion on my clothes plight and let me through! But the clothes and the pointing finger and flashing eyes had absolutely NO impact on the burly officer before me, who had obviously had a lot of practice on Mexicans and other poor languishing visa waiver offenders before me.

183

"YOU," he stated in no uncertain terms. "Wait over there!"

I shuffled back into the corner, looking up at the huge black and white picture that adorned the wall of the immigration office. It was a picture of nineteenth-century men and women who all looked, without exception, exceptionally grim. Almost out of a Stephen King movie. "Humph!" I thought. Maybe they TOO had been turned away and then photographed! "They also," I muttered "must have been victims of the visa waiver violations."

My children were glaring at me in a strange mixture of awe and fury.

No one else, of course, in our family was affected. Because they – *great heroes of the skies* – had, unlike me, FLOWN out of America and were *not* in breach of the visa waiver program. As for the now languishing Christian television prophet – she – great hero of the terra firma – great coward of the skies – had refused to fly 30,000 feet up in an aluminum tube at every opportunity she could get out of – where the temperature is minus 70 and you hurtle through the air at the grand speed of 500 mph. (My son insists on reading me the *exact* speed and Fahrenheit every five minutes, the downside of a vivid creative writing imagination.) I am so thrilled to say that after that experience I was delivered from my fear of flying and have crossed the oceans many, many times since!

However – this is now, that was then ... And there was only ONE person to blame for the situation at Rainbow Bridge, and that was Wendy Alec.

"YOU," the voice boomed again. I approached the glass booth again, this time my finger not pointing and my eyes not flashing, the dreadful truth dawning on me. Who needed the devil – when Wendy Alec could get kicked out of America all on her own initiative!

The immigration officer slammed my passport down on the counter. Rory was just brilliant as he is in these kind of situations, but however much he pleaded, this was the state and the Law was the Law.

This was America. I was British. I did not have an American Passport. And I had overstayed my time.

"You can all go back," the officer stated again. "But SHE can't cross the border!"

Dear friends, I have to tell you the truth. That day was one of the worst days of my life! My entire life seemed to flash before me. Now I had jeopardized the whole of GOD TV and its launch into America. And worse was to come. We phoned Steve Beik, our wonderful administrator who was also a lawyer. He in turn got hold of the officer in charge of Rainbow Bridge. This gentleman was far more compassionate. But the Law was the Law. I was banned from America. Our American lawyers weren't certain that I would *ever* be allowed back. I had visions of being stranded alone in England with Rory and the kids in Fredericksburg.

Our whole LIFE was in Virginia and DC now – all our belongings, clothes, home, furniture. Well, we celebrated Samantha's birthday woefully overlooking Niagara Falls – then got the first flight out from Toronto to Glasgow and then down to London. Just to add to this story, two weeks later, a dear friend popped into the house in Fredericksburg to make sure that it was alright, and found that the IRON had been left on! Oh Lord, we must have had an ANGEL standing over it! I didn't dare tell my parents or our colleagues what had happened. I just prayed fervently for the Father to have mercy on my sorry situation!

Well the American visa lawyers in London were brilliant. But my American future was still uncertain.

Within weeks Rory and I were standing with my new application in a long queue outside the American embassy.

"Only people who have appointments can go in!" the security officer declared, going down the queues.

"Oh Lord . . . " the coward whispered, "I don't want to go in alone as a visa waiver violator. Please let them not turn Rory away!" But I could hear the officer drawing nearer to us, coming down the line. He was polite but insistent.

"Only those with appointments." And I had an appointment (as the visa waiver violator!) but Rory surely didn't. Well the security officer got to us and suddenly smiled broadly.

"Why! It's Rory and Wendy of the GOD Channel – I don't believe it!" and without ANY further ado – he, an avid GOD TV viewer, let us BOTH through. How amazing and merciful our Father is even on our mistakes!

Once inside, we lined up in the "normal" renewing visa line. But when my turn came, the man behind the glass put my passport through his system, then shook his head. He looked at me strangely.

"You can't come in here," he said. "You have to go through to the CRIMINAL section."

I thought he was *joking!* But his face was stern. All color drained from my face.

"Through THERE," he pointed, looking at me again very strangely. Sternly. Later, we learned that the section is mainly reserved for drug smugglers and those of generally much greater crimes than visa waiver violations.

I was now a bona fide United States immigration criminal.

On our way out across the hall, a lovely lady accosted me and said, "I watch GOD TV all the time – I'm an intercessor – please pray for me I need a visa." I smiled wanly. In actual fact, *I* wanted to desperately clutch onto *her* jacket and say, "Pray *Pray* – I BEG you, pray for *me* – I'm going to the criminal section!" But instead we smiled nicely – like all good Christian television founders should – maybe a little wanly – and off we walked out of the normal visa section over to the more "austere" side of the embassy.

And sat.

And sat.

And sat for hours, watching as the offenders before me came and went. I watched, pale and trembling as I saw their visas refused. And still we sat. Over three hours had passed. Suddenly ALL the immigration officers went for lunch together, leaving all of us offenders staring at seven empty cubicles.

The disarming thought crossed my mind that maybe they disappeared to Brighton Beach every afternoon to teach us visa waiver offenders a lesson!

Never fear! After another hour of empty cubicles, the officers returned. I remember, in desperate boredom, staring at the huge poster up on the wall that read "25 million dollar reward for the capture of Osama Bin Laden." That would make a great project, I thought – a different angle for a Mission's Week! Imagine if all our viewers could go to Afghanistan and Asia and track him down. One of our viewers could capture Osama Bin Laden and donate the millions to GOD TV. We wouldn't need to produce a Mission's Week that year. Oh, that surely would have been wonderful!

But my grand Osama Mission's Week reveries were interrupted as my number was called. But not before the young woman before me who I could overhear had been living in Los Angeles for years was REFUSED entry ever again to the USA. She burst into loud sobs. They called my name. I dragged myself **reluctantly** up to the booth, feeling sick to my stomach.

The man studied my case and all the notes. He looked at my pitiful face. Then handed my passport back. "They can be a bit tough at the borders," he said gently. Then handed me my visa waiver forms.

"You mean I can go back?"

He nodded.

Oh what joy! What repentance! "From now on I will fly, Father!" I said to God. "I will fly!" What rejoicing that evening, and an admission of the whole story finally to my parents and friends.

187

And so, within days, we were on a plane back to Washington DC, this time for the final preparation of our USA launch.

There is one more addition to this story. And that is that on applying for our more permanent visas, which I am so thankful to say we now have, I was once again turned away and had to re-enter the criminal section with the whole FAMILY accompanying me! A story they don't easily let me forget!

This continued each time until this year, when I had an American Embassy breakthrough! When my passport was put through the scanner, I was, for the first time, allowed to stay in the normal visa line. The season had finally changed! For myself, I am just totally grateful to the Lord that He showed such mercy to me!

A lesson that I would never forget.

CHAPTER TWENTY-ONE

DISTRIBUTION

Well – WE ARRIVED BACK into Dulles Airport, in Washington DC, with great excitement in our hearts, believing the launch of GOD TV across America would be imminent. But after meeting after meeting, there was still no breakthrough with our distribution for the USA.

So many ministries were now excited about GOD TV coming to America, but we were not able to give them a *definite* date for our launch – as we still had no firm contracts for satellite or cable distribution in America.

We knew beyond any doubt that the platform that we needed to launch from was the DIRECT TV platform. It was a satellite platform that broadcast many different channels across the United States of America to over 14 million television households from the East to West Coasts, and we knew, for us, that it was the most effective way to start.

It was owned by Rupert Murdoch's company, who also owned the British satellite platform called Sky on which GOD TV had launched years before in England. But there was no breakthrough. Every door we pushed was closed to us. The answer from Direct TV was clear – there was NO channel available on Direct TV for GOD TV or ANY other channel for that matter until some years ahead.

And, once again, the cable operators would only take us seriously when we launched.

It was a challenging situation to say the least. We had moved our whole family to America. Our team was set up. We had premises in downtown Washington DC, a fledgling American regional office in Orlando, Florida – but *still* we could not BROADCAST our signal into the United States. We were beginning to sense that God's purposes for GOD TV in America were causing the devil to combat us on every turn. This was fierce opposition, as fierce as when we had first launched Christian television in England and Europe. And we just sensed in our spirits that the mandate of GOD TV for the United States of America was to be just as pivotal as the launch of GOD TV into Britain and Europe all those years before. But we needed God's direction and His breakthrough.

But we STILL had no broadcast platform in the United States.

We had already had to cancel two launch dates – and were fast becoming the laughingstock of our earthly ne'er-do-wells who would have been happy for us to flee from the shores of North America!

Meanwhile several Christian television channels in England appeared to be trying to take maximum advantage of our absence in Britain to attract our viewership to themselves, playing on the fact that GOD TV was no longer British as we had moved!

Oh – we seemed to be caught between a rock and a hard place both in England and America. But still we sensed deep inside that no matter the fight – we HAD to see this through.

We would trust God to preserve our place with our beloved viewers in England. We had hoped that they would understand our mission to the United States. But there were many rumors being propagated by those who would want to see us fail in England and many rumors in America that we were failing as we hadn't yet launched!

Many attacks on every front. But we had to stay the course and trust the Father to bring us through.

And here I just want to say – that our viewers in Great Britain have been incredible. On our return, we found that many, many of them did understand the spiritual nature of the battle. The wonderful thing about our GOD TV viewers all across the world is that they TOO have a heart for missions and evangelism. They too want us as GOD TV to go, be obedient and preach the Gospel to every creature.

But far greater than human opposition was *the fierce opposition in the spirit*.

All around America, friends and ministries were waiting in anticipation for GOD TV to launch. And two and a half years after landing in the United States, we still had no breakthrough. And in the natural – we faced continual "NOs."

It looked as though there was no glimmer of hope on the horizon.

"...BUT GOD..." The still small voice of the Holy Spirit whispered.

We were now seriously considering finding ways straight to Rupert Murdoch's office in New York. But our Father in Heaven is so great. And when it is His sovereign and divine purpose – there is no devil or demon or man who can stop his plan – maybe delay for a short season but not stop the plans and purposes of Almighty God.

And so we had to stand on the word God gave us – "LAUNCH GOD TV INTO AMERICA."

But even though we were experiencing one of the greatest battles of our lives in the United States, God was blessing other areas

191

of the ministry in an incredible manner. We continued to press onward on every front to broadcast the Gospel to more territories as we felt so strongly in our spirits that time was short.

At this point one of the greatest doors for the utterance of the Gospel of the Lord Jesus Christ was about to open up to GOD TV – the door to CHINA. Many, many secular and Christian broadcasters had been trying for years to enter China. We had received prophecies earlier that GOD TV would broadcast into China and receive favor everywhere that Chinese was spoken.

The first door was about to open. To Hong Kong, the gateway to China.

By a divine miracle of God, GOD TV was invited onto the foremost cable operator in Hong Kong – Hong Kong Cable.

We shared about this incredible opportunity to our viewers immediately from our studios in Washington DC. Our viewers in Great Britain and beyond rose to the cause in an astounding way. They were simply amazing! And in under a weekend, we were able to raise the money for a year's broadcast to Hong Kong and secure the platform.

Rory and our head of Distribution, Bo Sander, traveled to Hong Kong and were actually *in* Hong Kong Cable as the very first GOD TV broadcasts beamed out into Hong Kong, China. It was historic! – a momentous occasion in the Spirit!

Since then, GOD TV has beamed out its signal into Hong Kong twenty-four hours a day every day for over two years to a staggering *two million Chinese viewers*. A great and timely door of utterance.

We do not know how long the door will remain open. We do not take this door of utterance lightly, but thank the Lord for every day that the darkness over this nation can be pierced with the Gospel.

Meanwhile, our broadcasts in Europe were strengthening substantially and the signal of GOD TV was now saturating the nations.

Again, at this time the Lord opened up some significant doors for the proclamation of the Gospel.

We were now broadcasting to over one and a half million viewers on the leading satellite platform, the TPS platform in France. Then the leading Scandinavian platforms VIASAT and Canal Digital opened up to us to broadcast daily to over *five* million viewers across Sweden, Norway and Denmark, an incredible breakthrough, thanks to the tireless efforts of Simon Jacobsen, Scandinavia's Regional director and Bo Sander our dedicated Head of GOD TV's distribution. These platforms were the equivalent of the USA DIRECT TV's of France and Scandinavia.

Germany's expansion followed swiftly. The GOD Channel had already been on ASTRA for many years for several hours a day, but in January 2003 the broadcasts were extended to eight hours a day on the ASTRA satellite and a German office was set up to respond to the broadcasts. (From 15 March 2006, its coverage increased to twenty-four hours!) Glory to God! We were starting to significantly affect the European TV marketplace.

GOD TV was growing rapidly across Europe and was now being received by millions across Albania, Austria, Belarus, Belgium, Bosnia and Herzegovina, Bulgaria, Croatia, Cyprus, Czech Republic, Denmark, Finland, France, Germany, Greece, Hungary, Holland, Iceland, Ireland, Kazakhstan, Latvia, Liechtenstein, Lithuania, Luxembourg, Malta, Netherlands, Norway, Poland, Portugal, Romania, Russia, Slovakia, Slovenia, Spain, Sweden, Switzerland, Ukraine and the United Kingdom on a daily basis. Meanwhile, our satellite coverage now reached even further East to include Turkey, Afghanistan, Pakistan, Azerbaijan and the former Soviet Union.

Also in Great Britain, we were at this time not only broadcasting on the Sky Platform but were also the only UK Christian Channel to broadcast on *all* British cable operators, which also included Southern and Northern Ireland, and on the Isle of Wight.

It was also during this perplexing season in America that the Lord started to open up a great door of utterance to one of the great heartbeats of GOD TV – the Middle East.

We have such a burning passion to reach both the Arab and the Jewish inhabitants of the Middle East. In the prophecy that prophet Jonathan David brought to us so many years past, before we had even launched GOD TV, he prophesied that the Middle East would open up to us – and today we see the fulfillment of that prophecy every day.

After our global broadcast from Washington DC at the beginning of the war in Iraq, GOD TV was one of the very first broadcasters – secular or Christian, to beam into Iraq with an estimated 30 to 40 percent of all Iraqi homes now able to view GOD TV. We were so deeply moved that in the midst of tragedy and conflict, that GOD TV could be there as a lifeline and that the Gospel of the Lord Jesus could be preached.

It was during this challenging time that GOD TV started to broadcast across the Middle East into Algeria, Bahrain, Egypt, Iraq, Iran, Israel, Jordan, Kuwait, Lebanon, Libya, Morocco, Oman, Qatar, Saudi Arabia, Syria: Damascus, Tunisia, Turkey, United Arab Emirates and Yemen.

We regularly receive deeply touching reports from many, many viewers in these regions that GOD TV is literally a lifeline in their homes. We thank the Lord for this great and awesome privilege. Again, we do not take it lightly. *Then in March 2005*, Australia opened up to us and we sense in our spirits that the Lord is about to open an even greater door of utterance in Australia for GOD TV. We love Australia and New Zealand.

All this incredible distribution breakthrough in the uttermost parts of the earth – but still no distribution breakthrough in America – the Gates of the United States seemed like brass!

During this time, we were invited to a have dinner with a very influential minister and his wife at the Hays Adam Hotel in Washington DC. Our schedule was so packed and that night, we still had to drive the 50 miles back to Fredericksburg, back to our children. Our dinner meeting was held up – with tremendous traffic problems. We sat in the lounge of the Hays Adam – till 8.00 then till 8.30 and decided that we would have to leave by 9.00. But we felt in our spirits this was an important connection, so we waited.

It was a wonderful evening with a great man and woman of God. They were both so very gracious and so generous of heart. We were so blessed in our spirits to meet them and we knew the connection was significant in God for the future. But that night, the conversation went no further than possible airtime opportunities on GOD TV.

During the dinner, the minister had said. "Do you know Rupert Murdoch?" And I had wanted to cry out – "No – do YOU know him??" in desperation. But I restrained my desperation and instead just smiled politely like a polite Christian ministry woman was supposed to. Before we continue with this story, I need to say that in our entire conversation, the issue of DIRECT TV never came up.

A week later, dear friends, Rory received a call while he was traveling in Africa. Oh – beloved – this is about God's supreme hand of grace and favor and goodness. This is one of the most sovereign miracles that Rory and I and GOD TV have ever experienced in our lives, the fruit of which shall only be revealed as destiny unfolds in the years ahead.

This same minister asked Rory if he knew a good media lawyer as he had **JUST BEEN GIVEN A WHOLE TWENTY-FOUR-HOUR CHANNEL on DIRECT TV.**

This was just incredible. Well, media lawyers are something we are never short of knowing – but the story ends like this. This very precious God-fearing couple prayed – and God directed them to give GOD TV the CHANNEL on DIRECT TV so that GOD TV could LAUNCH into America. Praise God for their faithfulness and obedience – I believe that they will only realize in Heaven what they truly did that day for America's destiny and for the Lord.

As I write this, I want to cry as my spirit is overwhelmed with the goodness and the sovereignty of a mighty, *mighty* incredible God and the obedience of His faithful servants who heard His voice . . . the one who hears our prayers – who knows our needs – who plans our lives in the most intricate of details – who never ever fails us, the God who saw the ferocious opposition to GOD TV launching into America, who in His divine and sovereign plan sat us opposite the man who GOD knew was to be given a whole CHANNEL on DIRECT TV the next *week* after we met him and his wife.

It is one of the greatest miracles we have ever experienced. And on that note, another amazing miracle as we entered the USA; the facilities/broadcast house that we had first rented studio and uplink space from in Washington DC, and had conducted our call to Prayer in Iraq from Washington DC, had gone into receivership. To cut a long story short, a large Christian organization actually BOUGHT it for us and gave it, lock, stock and barrel to GOD TV as a *gift*.

This miracle meant that by October 2005, GOD TV owned its own broadcast production house with cameras, galleries, mobile production trucks with uplink/downlink capabilities, edit suites as well as a fully-fledged transmission center . . . all in Washington DC. We were able to kit out our galleries and studios with USA equipment. We now also had a duplicate transmission center in the heart of Washington DC that could be used for Israel if required.

To top it all, in the overall package, we had also acquired eight broadcast locations with spectacular White House backgrounds from the roof of the Chamber of Commerce and even our own spot on the White House lawn!

Now our clients included the BBC, FOX, NBC, Bloomberg, Nippon TV, APTN, SKY NEWS just to name a few – the Lord is great! And now the Lord would say to you as you read today:

Child – beloved child – even as you yourself have cried out to Me in certain areas of your life for breakthrough, know this. That I am the God who sees, that I am the God who hears, that I am the God who answers prayers by FIRE. And the Lord would say to you – My child – I am the lifter of your head – and even though your hands have hung down because the vision and the dream that was birthed in your spirit has been so long in coming to pass, I tell you this day beloved – that you are not forgotten by Me. And even in a MOMENT, says the Lord God of Hosts, even as in a MOMENT, I shall turn the situation – I shall turn the circumstance – I shall breathe upon the dead bones. And, My child, that which I have spoken to you in secret shall be birthed and shall come forth into the daylight. And that which you have seen in your closet shall come forth into the visible realm. For I AM the God of sudden-lies – for those who worship Me – and pursue My purposes and who seek My face. So lift up your head, My child – lift up your head. For it is I, the Lord your God, who comes toward you this day and this hour. For surely you SHALL see the hand of the Living God in your situation.

CHAPTER TWENTY-TWO

THE MAYFLOWER BECKONS – CALL TO PLYMOUTH, ENGLAND

W E HAD A SECURE CHANNEL on DIRECT TV – but now the very *earliest* launch date they could give us was October 2006. And we were set to launch in October 2005. But there was no earlier opportunity. NOW we had to put off the launch into America AGAIN for yet another *whole year*. This was an immense challenge for us.

But we had to trust that God Himself had preordained a specific day and hour that He had ordained for GOD TV to start to broadcast its signal into America.

We had no idea what was ahead.

We were to discover much later that 1 October 2006 was the date that had been set aside by many of the most influential ministers across America to pray each year for the peace of Israel. They had prayed and felt that the Lord had directed them to put aside the FIRST SUNDAY of each October to pray for the peace of Jerusalem and the peace of Israel.

In the year 2006 – that Sunday fell on 1 OCTOBER – the exact date of Yom Kippur and when GOD TVs first broadcast was transmitted from our broadcast center in Mount Zion across the United States of America!

It was also our eleventh birthday and the opening and dedication of our Broadcast center and Jerusalem studio.

Oh, how jealous God the Father is over His supreme hand and purpose. And so many times we all walk by faith, not understanding the complete picture – but our Father always knows. And, Oh, what thanks we must give to our amazing incredible GOD TV family of viewers in Great Britain and around the world – they stood with us for America through thick and thin, never wavering.

But back to our story. Well, after our tenth birthday celebration at David's Citadel in Jerusalem, we flew back to England. And the strangest thing happened. Rory and I started to feel a stirring towards moving back to England. At first we rebuked it, thinking it was our own flesh, but on our return to Fredericksburg, a beautiful town we were completely settled in, it was as though the Lord had sovereignly shut down something in our spirit. It was unprecedented. We could not explain what was happening on the inside of us. We had just bought a small farmholding in Fredericksburg – we *loved* America. This was also the very first house in England or the USA that was to be our OWN. We would have to give it up.

But, it seemed that still small whisper was stirring us up like Abraham again. Our whole life was in America – we had planned to stay there for our future. Our children were being schooled there. But it seemed that the Lord was blowing on us by His Holy Spirit again. But if we WERE to return to England – where was it to be?

We knew beyond any doubt that it wasn't the North this time. And now the Lord said that He would bring us in by a different gate. And somehow Plymouth kept stirring in our hearts. Our British regional director Chris Cole and his lovely wife Kerry lived there and we knew they loved it. But that wasn't reason enough for us not to look any further. Well, we'd never even BEEN to Plymouth but somehow the Lord never let it go, so I started to scour the internet looking for houses. We visited Plymouth a month later, saw our house by faith and eventually, after a few obstacles and challenges, our brave little pioneer, Samantha was in England starting her schooling.

On 14 February 2006 – on what we believed to be the Word of the Lord, we packed up our belongings once more and left the shores of the United States.

Rory, Christian and I left New York and flew to Israel to do a live broadcast from Jerusalem, then we flew to London and after a few days went straight up to Sunderland to broadcast Mission's Week.

Oh yes – but the life of a pioneer is not always smooth. We literally lived out of suitcases for NINE weeks before we could settle in Cornwall. But I was able to spend wonderful time with my beloved earthly father – Doc Koefman – who was ninety-one. Eight weeks after we landed and two days after we moved into our home in England – Daddy died. How wonderful of the Lord to arrange for me to spend so much time with my beloved earthly father in his last days.

The very last words that he spoke to me, although he could barely talk, were: "I love you, my darling."

Rory was in Jerusalem on the Thursday evening that we were transmitting the Seder Meal LIVE from the Upper Room. The broadcast started at 8.30 p.m. Daddy, born a Jew, a true son of Abraham, died at exactly 8.40 p.m.

His great friend, also ninety-one, an Anglican canon, never came to my parent's house at night. But he felt compelled by the Holy Spirit to come that night to watch the GOD TV broadcast. As Daddy was taking his last breath, the canon stood by his bed saying Daddy's favorite prayer, the Lord's Prayer. In the middle of the Lord's prayer, Daddy who had glaucoma and was blind, opened his eyes wide as could be – wide – wide – then he died.

And although it was a time of great sadness, it was a time of such joy, that the Lord had taken him home on Passover. The relationship that I have with my incredible heavenly Father today, I owe so greatly to my wonderful earthly father, Doc Koefman – full of grace and wisdom, compassion and strength, an eternal gift from the Father Himself. And the greatest thing in his life – his immense, over-riding, all-encompassing love of His Almighty God.

There is another little family cameo here, which I know Daddy wouldn't mind me writing, as he was endowed with the most hysterical dry sense of humor.

It could literally have come out of a "soap!"

As my father was getting older, he wanted to discuss more practical things: e.g. HIS **burial**, what should be on the gravestone etc., a lengthy source of *long and loud* debates in his household, where every man and his dog added their own opinion.

These steaming debates would filter across the garden fence in summer to all the long-suffering neighbors (luckily they are all great friends of many years) of the sedate Dorset community!

Daddy wanted to be cremated. As a medical doctor, that was his wish. That was okay – that is not where the debate started.

Then, instead of being buried in England, in Dorset (the expectation of most around him, in the local Church of England gravesite just a few miles away), he decided that he wanted to be buried in the place where he had found the most peace on earth.

It just so happened to be "Capernaum" by the Sea of Galilee in *Northern Israel*. (We *did* actually have a conversation on the status of his ashes in the case of a Syrian attack!)

Daddy had sat under a tree there looking out onto the Sea of Galilee, he told us, and more than any other place on earth (he was exceptionally well traveled), his love for that place had remained with him his whole life.

Great, Daddy. This just happens to be the most prime real estate in Israel, every square inch bought up by Christian pilgrims. Ahem.

The size of the gravestone grew and grew. My mother, practical and utilitarian, wanted a small unostentatious little plaque – a memorial stone.

Daddy wanted a gravestone.

Each member of the family had different ideas.

Then Daddy started dictating WHAT he wanted on the gravestone.

He wanted first and foremost the line "I LOVE GOD"

Then "Before Abraham was, I am."

Then the first commandment written out in *full*.

By this time my mother saw the plaque going west, but it didn't stop there. THEN Daddy got enthusiastic – he considered his great grandchildren and future generations and looked at my mother with a glint in his eye.

"You must put – doctor – medical doctor . . . " he hesitated, "and Captain" he continued earnestly, " . . . in the United States Army." (He was stationed in the USA army as head surgeon of the bomber division in England during the Second World War, as my grandfather had an American Passport, having run away from Poland to New York in the 1880s!) " . . . and my medals . . . "

My mother was staring at him in utter disbelief.

"You *must list* my medals . . . " He stared at my mother sternly, " . . . For the grandchildren!"

Daddy's memorial stone had now turned from a small plaque to a gravestone – and was rapidly burgeoning into a mammoth mausoleum-like tomb.

AND he wanted everyone who visited him to place a stone on his gravestone like Schindler's List. (Not easy to do on a plaque!)

The story is still in process. The very **week** that we were going out to Israel for three days as a family to search for a resting place for Daddy in Tiberius, Galilee, the Israeli–Lebanon War broke out!! And TIBERIUS and Northern Israel was rained on with MISSILES!

We have forbidden my mother from taking a trip on a boat in Galilee and throwing Daddy's ashes out onto the water there, as she finally threatened to do in exasperation. (We will keep careful eyes on her pockets when we visit Galilee!)

So, Daddy's ashes are still waiting patiently in the conservatory of my mother's house, in a far more peaceful part of the world called Dorset in England, where missiles don't fly.

But on a serious note, we will find a wonderful place and give him a wonderful stone as a memorial to his immense love for his God, Almighty God. As I write we are looking along Galilee for a call center and retreat for our GOD TV viewers – maybe it will be there. He would so love that as he LOVED what we were doing for the Lord!

But back to Plymouth, England.

Well – after being remote from many of our vision and creative team for nearly three years, we decided to create what we have since christened "AREA 51," named by our hardy senior Network planner (you can see we're all media animals!) – which is GOD TV's RESEARCH and DEVELOPMENT division. We were so blessed.

Many of our closest vision and creative team moved down to Plymouth to be with us. As I write our studio/offices in Plymouth are bursting at the seams with the pressures of a television launch! Stresses, strains and unimaginable excitement as we prepare for the American launch. We have just received at long last Planning Permission for our Plymouth Studio – which is such a blessing as at present Rory and I have no way of going LIVE and no studios to broadcast from.

Our edit suites have arrived, the walls are being painted and our team are plumbing in edit suites and library servers. The boardroom is crammed with all of us around the boardroom table holding communication meetings, design meetings, schedule plannings, programing, commissioning, creative service policies, business strategy – and all of this by faith because as it has been in this season – we don't know precisely where our launch budget is coming from as we need all GOD TV's money that comes in just to run our monthly budgets!

But we continue by faith to do, to stretch, to multi-skill, to roll up our sleeves to create a channel glorifying to God – a channel that will reach the lost and hurting, that will equip and mobilize the Church.

And of course Plymouth is the home of the Mayflower Steps – where the pilgrims departed all those generations before to impact the New World. And like our forefathers before us – we humbly give ourselves at GOD TV to serve the United States of America – ourselves as visionaries – our fantastic teams – our viewers across the world, we know are all ready and poised to serve YOU, beloved America – in any and every way we can. Our regional offices are now established in Orlando, Florida. And as we launch – precious American friend – know that you have our hearts. Our commitment, our passion, our talents and our giftings we lay at His feet – that the Lord Jesus Christ Himself will break us and our team as he broke the bread and fed the thousands – so too says the Lord – I will in turn break GOD TV and feed the hungry the starving the yearning hearts all across America that My people may fed, that My children may be fed, that My eagles may be fed.

And know that we stand with you, America, in the years to come – that all across the world we may rise as a great and fearsome spiritual army in these end times against the works of the devil and do the works of our Lord Jesus Christ – to glorify the Father and to preach the Gospel of His Son – to every nation. Then shall the end come. So be it.

CHAPTER TWENTY-THREE

RORY AND WENDY – ONE NEW MAN

WELL – THIS IS TO BE an interesting chapter. Rory and I together truly operate as "ONE NEW MAN!" Not only have we got the mix of Jew and Gentile, we are both apostolic and prophetic.

Rory is CEO of GOD TV as a King with a strong apostolic, building anointing, whereas I strongly lean to prophet-evangelist and my role in the network is the televisual side – the creative and programing – that is in laymen's terms – everything that you actually see on your television screen.

Rory spends his life on the blackberry and mobile phone, networking, building, deal making and raising money. He travels consistently in a never ending very grueling schedule across the globe to GOD TV's regional offices, to Africa to break the ground for transmitters, to India to film updates and empower our teams, to America to network and set things in motion for our American launch and distribution, to meet with ministers from all across the globe ... the list continues.

The greatest pressure in his days is the continual lack of ready funds to be able to continue to build the network. Our wondrous long-suffering financial director, Paul le Druillenac, phones him (normally every Christmas or every time we're about to try to have a family holiday!). It gets worse – normally we need about a million pounds extra every six weeks. Although our viewers are amazing and so many fulfill their pledges during our Mission Weeks (telethons) – still there are times when, because pledges during Mission's Week haven't been fulfilled, the ministry suffers.

I have seen Rory carry on his shoulders the most terrible intense pressure of finance in this ministry because, at the end of the day, he is the one who has to find the MONEY.

I normally am pretty relaxed when we need millions – except on rare occasions when it has got beyond the beyond (when I have wanted to actually get on a plane and FLY away – and that is pretty miraculous!). But at the end of the day – the buck and the pressure stops with Rory, not with me. And I ADMIRE him SO much for his unending capacity to endure and to push on no matter the circumstances.

It is an apostolic gift and I have seen my husband grow in God and in the authority of his call with every passing year – and it is a phenomenal thing to watch. He is a great leader and commander of GOD TV's army.

As for me – my role is to oversee and create the television aspect of GOD TV as Network Controller and creative/artistic director – from the Network schedules through to the Programing, Acquisitions, Commissioning and Creative Services. I spend my days (and nights) before a new launch on the blackberry and computer planning GOD TV programing, upgrading the GOD TV schedules, commissioning, creating and editing with my *fantastic* creative and vision teams the creative look and content that reaches your screens through GOD TV's programing and on-air look.

Included in my job-spec is scripting and producing GOD TV's Mission's Weeks, our birthday and launch televisual events, finding new anointed talent, developing our youth programing, commissioning the GOD TV global conferences – deciding what's live and what's to be live to tape. Yes – it goes on and on – the hardest thing for me this year was to try to cram the writing of my second novel *MESSIAH* into a few weeks.

Oh guys, I nearly burnt myself out – I was literally writing day and night – never resting – week and weekends. By the time I had to start curving creatively for our huge launch into your amazing continent of North America, I was sitting with an almost complete words-on-paper manuscript with at least ten re-edits to do. So we had to make a decision to delay the novel until after the launch into America.

And as you can see in my excess time during the pre launch – I am upgrading what you are reading now, dear reader – the ten-year-old *Against All Odds* manuscript especially for YOU!! Next year I'm going to SLEEP for a month!

But Rory and I wouldn't swap it for anything – and God DOES manage to bring us in balance!

The amazing thing is that in the Body of Christ sometimes the hardest thing is for apostles and prophets to work together. But you know that in God, we believe that the apostolic-prophetic team is purposed to be by the Lord one of the greatest mix of call and anointing for any visionary work. One pulls, the other pushes – then the next day the tables are turned.

There are times that Rory goes so fast on issues that I feel should be slow, then goes SO – oh so VERY slowly on issues that I feel we should be racing on – and *VICE VERSA!!* And we have both found time after time over the years that this juxtaposition creates a TRUE balance of the timings and the sovereign purposes of God in our ministry.

We feel very, very blessed to have as our pastor and also as a trustee of GOD TV the wonderful wise and discerning Francis Frangipane. (He also has a very dry and amazing sense of humor!) A pastor to pastors.

We met dear Pastor Francis over a dinner after he had been on one of our shows in England about six years ago. He shared with us that the Lord had put it on his heart to pray for us every day and this was the beginning of a long and growing relationship. We are privileged that a man who teaches so much on Christlikeness and who has such a deep and genuine desire to be Christlike himself, carries an oversight of our souls.

As one prophet once declared over us, Rory and I come from opposite sides, each bringing the same good thing. And now that we've been married twenty years this January, we can honestly say – it's never been better. We are best friends, can't live without each other – tuned in to each other's minds and joined at the hip – God has done an incredible thing. We've had our ups. We've had our downs! But we have worked so many, many things out through the years and I can honestly say – that what you see … nowadays is TRULY what you get.

Rory is the Visionary – the Builder. His passion is to build brick by brick a strong media structure, its application in television, film and publishing with a foundation that is strong and sure and will last through this generation and generations to come. I am prophet, evangelist, an artist, primarily a creator-innovator operating inspirationally. My passion is to create media product – the output of which translates into television, film and books – and to equip the Church and to reach a jaded, cynical secular world who hunger for the things of God but just don't *necessarily* know it!

Prophetic utterances over our lives have called Rory an "Apostle to the Media" and myself a "Prophet to the Media." Our primary call is MEDIA.

One creates the product/content. The other builds the infrastructure for the product/content, although many times we are known to cross-pollinate!

The one thing we are so very, very grateful to the Lord for is the tremendous GRACE upon our lives to withstand a great deal of pressure and mental hardship and stress. Things can be horrific, falling down around our heads. But the next morning through the grace of God, we'll bounce back onto our feet and say, "But what IF!!"

Also – where one of us is weak, the other normally remains strong. For example, at certain emotional pressure, I could collapse and become an emotional basketcase except for the Lord's grace to assist me through, whereas Rory will say – "Just deal with it!"

Well, guys – what do you do when there's no option but to deal with it? – so the prophet has no option but to climb out of her languishing prophetic stupor and pity party (fuelled by a vivid creative imagination) and just DEAL with it!

How I used to hate that in our early years of marriage – but I have found that it is SO good for my temperament to have that balance from my partner. On the other hand, Rory may be reeling under the money pressures of the ministry, but I can cope with some of the more practical challenges like those issues fairly easily. (Though I haven't quite got to saying "Deal with it!" to him!)

So, we have discovered that the inherent weaknesses in one another have actually become a helper to the one struggling. In our early years I would think Rory was harsh and unsympathetic. Today, I realize that I would have spent a *lot* longer in the "grovel pit" without that unfailing choleric assistance! Again vice versa. I am pretty laid back in other areas where Rory would feel the intense pressure of ministry.

I think the greatest lesson I have learned through the years is that what one may initially consider as one's spouse's weakness, through the years, can actually develop into their greatest strength.

We find that so often God, by His eternal design, places people together in marriage who are a refining agent to each other and who complement each other. And that it is IN this process, if one yields to it, that God truly can be glorified.

And yes, we do lead a very normal, family life. The toothpaste top stays off, no one puts the toilet roll back in the holder, clothes can lay strewn all across the bathroom floor (as though waiting for the Butler Jeeves to pick them up ... except for one minor fact – the Butler Jeeves does not visit our house!).

As I've been writing, our Ridgeback has just eaten Samantha's sandal and a slipper in the bathroom! I am so grateful to say that I've found a local lady who cleans a few hours a week and will do a wash – as Rory arrives back from trips with PILES of clothes! Our wonderful children are growing up so fast. They both love the Lord. Sammy is now fifteen and Christian eleven. Sammy loves to sing and excels in drama and music. She is extremely creative and has her father's natural leadership ability.

Christian is a really well balanced child. He is endowed with grace as his grandfather was. He plays drums, is tremendously creative, and has his mother's vivid imagination. Maybe he'll direct later.

They've both inherited writing abilities (from me) and musical skills (from Rory) but most importantly, they love the Lord. It was prophesied over them that they are both called to media and will do twice what Rory and I have done! They are completely real and have ridden the pioneering road with us like God's great troopers and we know the Lord will bless them greatly for their faithfulness.

We are so very proud of them.

We have a cat, two fantastic, albeit wild, Ridgebacks (which is like having seven non-"behaved" normal dogs!) and now, courtesy of the local farmer, a bevy of cows and sheep right outside our front door. Praise be to the Lord for great things He has done!

CHAPTER TWENTY-FOUR

MISSION'S WEEK (GOD TV'S TELETHON)

WELL – MISSION'S WEEK – what a story we have to tell!

I will try and give you the background as best as I can. For the first seven years of GOD TV's broadcasts in the United Kingdom, in the midst of having to pay for our distribution in the UK and in Europe, we were not allowed by the British regulators to appeal for funds on air. After we moved our operation to Spain in 2002, we were out of the British jurisdiction and under European Law and eventually after much prayer felt that God had now given us permission to ask our viewers in England and around the world to participate.

So we started to produce a GOD TV Mission's Week that would play out twice a year in April and October.

It was a terrifying prospect to do this in Great Britain at the time and it took every ounce of courage that Rory and I possessed to see it through. Firstly, Great Britain was renowned among global Christian circles as being the one of the least forthcoming nations in the world to ever give to a Christian cause. Britain gave generously to any Third

World cause and to the poor, but when it came for asking for money to preach the Gospel, there was something in our British psyche that felt that it was "unpalatable."

Secondly, ministries from around the world had often viewed Britain as being stingy and reluctant givers.

Thirdly, there was a powerful spirit of "lack" and "cynicism" over the nation. And it was a spirit that was going to rise up against anyone who dared oppose it.

But we knew it was the season to enter into.

We also had the intense conviction in our hearts that some of the most generous and joy-filled giving in the world was going to come from the nation of Great Britain, that although the devil had labeled Great Britain when it came to finances, "What good can come out of Nazareth?" God had other plans. The Father had a twinkle in his eye and was actually going to *use* Great Britain in this season to literally proclaim the Gospel around the world – one of her foremost God-ordained calls and a well from the past that the Lord wanted reopened! We knew that the very act of thousands upon thousands of people giving to the cause of Christ was literally going to break Satan's stronghold over the finances of our viewers and over the spirit of lack and hoarding over the nation. Our viewers had always been amazing, but still – it was not going to be an easy ride.

So with great trepidation, in 2002, we broadcast our first Mission's Week. And our viewers rose so generously to the challenge and in five days we raised over 1.2 million pounds ($2 million) in gifts and pledges.

Dear friend, if you were one of those first givers, it might amaze you to know that the story of how you and our GOD TV viewers in Great Britain gave that Mission's Week resounded around the United States of America. People could simply NOT believe that that amount of money had been given by our viewers for the proclamation of the Gospel.

It was a dent in Satan's hold over the finances of Great Britain and Europe. But I personally didn't find it easy to ask for money. Maybe I am too British. I had grown up in a family where it was important to be self-sufficient – where you earned your own wage. And now – I was thrust into a situation where each evening it sometimes felt to me that we were literally thrown to the wolves, now, our beloved Britain, by that I mean the demonic spirits who rose against us!

I remember one Spring Partner Week when we actually started with a big NOUGHT above our heads for partners. Oh my gosh, I wanted to sink through the floor for the first two hours. Rory is a real trooper; he knows that it is essential to the foundations of GOD TV to build these foundations.

I, on the other hand, was praying desperately for a sympathetic multi-millionaire to suddenly drive up and drop a huge check in our hands! Then I could cancel Mission's Week!

I think the worst thing for me was that I could literally sense the battle for the airwaves in this area. I could vividly see Onslow (from *Keeping Up Appearances* on BBC America!) saying with folded arms, glaring to the television set. "Oh it's THEM – the GOD channel – they're asking for MONEY again!" before switching over on the remote!

And the "country casuals" set sipping tea and murmuring, "It's really distasteful, dear – all this asking for money. Tut! Tut!"

Another challenge for me is the immense drain on production resources that a Mission's Week entails. It is such a huge production; I have to take everyone off the vital production projects at hand and refocus them for the Week.

The videotape inserts that you watch have to be commissioned weeks in advance from all over the world, then filmed and finally edited. We have a small, incredibly talented production team and our wonderful Network Planning multi-skilled wonder team. Somehow we all manage to keep the twenty-four-hour broadcast program content going while we all concentrate on Mission's Week. Because it is a visionary Holy Spirit event, I write the scripts, commission the video tapes needed, select the content and by the time we open on the first night, I feel like I want to fall off the end of the gleaming white couch in a demented heap.

Meanwhile, MISTER Alec arrives, fresh as a daisy – wonderful master of ceremonies and host that he is – because he is just *fantastic!* Meanwhile I – who often can't hold a sentence together too accurately on screen – I'm producing/directing from the floor, changing the script minute by minute as we go – as generally after the first hour, things fall apart! I end up looking like some white-washed hag on the end of a white couch muttering incoherently into my direct line into the gallery! "That's the WRONG VT! WHERE are the guys in the UK? – WHY aren't they at the map? THAT'S the WRONG strap onscreen – get it OOOFFF! scrub the next VT – Go to Rory at the wide screen..." And so it goes on and on...

Well – in Newcastle, we finish at 11.00 p.m., sometimes midnight, then rush to Chinatown for dinner – the only open restaurant in Newcastle – and sit with a laptop writing the following day's script at 2.00 a.m. in the morning EVERY night.

Television is a grueling relentless beast – and Christian television, dear friends, is no exception!

But thank the Lord for our incredible, faithful wonderful GOD TV family who literally have stuck with us through thick and thin, through all the ups and downs. We are so very grateful to the Lord for our Angel Partners.

They will only truly know in eternity what they have done. And great, very great will be their reward.

Well our Mission's Weeks continued into 2003 then 2004. And it was in 2005 that the battle *really* began. Our viewers were used to us asking for financial assistance but we now had opposition from *other* channels in Britain who it seemed were intent on using our Mission's

Week Appeals against us in order to gain favor in our viewers' eyes. It seemed that they thought by making us appear the big bad older brother, their own agendas would be promoted.

Forgotten was the reality that while most channels in the UK were only two or three years old, we had only **started** Mission's Weeks when we had already been broadcasting for SEVEN years, and that in fact – our EARLY bills – when we had to pay for ANALOGUE distribution – were probably five times as much as these same channels pay today for DIGITAL. And we had walked by FAITH.

Oh, but we have had some memorable moments...

There was the time that, as we went on air, the power literally went out, all our equipment went down, and there were other times when satellite links went down, let alone the occasion when the **FBI** drew up outside the Washington offices!

These are many *many* stories that we still can't share – maybe in a twentieth anniversary book! And the Mission's Week of 2006 when we arrived back in Sunderland and were gatecrashed LIVE by what we eventually discovered to be a Channel Four crew (one of the UK's main terrestrial television channels – similar to ABC here) for a rather dubious documentary program.

Well – to backtrack – we had walked off the plane back into London into a barrage of secular media. The prince of the Power of the Air knew that we had stepped back into this country. But God had given Rory and me a DIRECT word. We were NOT to seek publicity. This was NOT God's timing to profile the Channel. We were to refuse all interviews and all publicity until a later time when God would be glorified through it.

So, instead of going after media opportunities, we kept turning them away.

It got so intense and several journalists from the British tabloids continued to pursue us relentlessly, one eventually offering GOD TV

5,000 pounds ($8,000) from his very influential British newspaper if we were to allow him or a crew of his choice to follow Rory and me around during Mission's Week. Well, we knew what the Lord had said and with our previous long experience of the cut-throat British media, we refused the offer immediately. We continue to keep a low profile until the season that the Lord has ordained comes.

We've also had such fun behind the scenes! Even in the hardest times when we wanted to fall through the floor because money was coming in at times **really** slowly. We were at the height of Mission's Week **exhaustion**, when we had degenerated into stuffing doughnuts (Chocolate Krispy Kremes! – we were in our Washington DC studios) and hot chocolate on live TV to ease the multiple pressures! And in our semi delirium, we all envisioned having 'Mission's Week' Police, led by our dear Johnny Woodrow, where we went in and handcuffed people to give in desperation! Oh forgive us! Mission's Week leaves us in a state of near-paralysis!

I finally collapsed half on air, half off in giggles, when Rory called **again** for that "elusive" millionaire to phone! (We had received words from ministers of the Gospel from over five years ago, that there is a multi-millionaire out there who will give a million dollars to GOD TV on a Mission's Week.)

We call for this millionaire to ring in every single Mission's Week – twice a year – but *this* time, I was so overtired, that when Rory mentioned it again (for the fifth year – tenth time) – I completely collapsed – it felt like we were "waiting for Godot!!!" (We've been waiting for THAT phone call since we started Mission's Week! But you know, no matter the giggles, we'll STILL stand in faith that one day we'll get a call from a viewer pledging one million dollars!)

Oh, how we love you. Please dear friends, know our hearts behind the scenes. We will NEVER take advantage. We will do our

UTMOST to obey and always hear the Lord. To all of you, our partners, our Angels, what can Rory and I say but that you are just the most incredible blessing to us and to GOD TV. And how well we know that this is echoed by ALL our GOD TV teams around the world. We love you – we honor you. Without you, millions of people across India, Africa, Hong Kong, Australia, Nepal, Germany – the list goes on and on – would never have heard the Gospel of our Lord Jesus Christ.

The road has been hard. There has been many a pothole (hundred foot ditch) along the way. But the fire and the flame that God the Father birthed in us over eleven years ago, has never faltered, has never grown dim.

We love you. We are here to serve you. We bless your lives, your families, your marriages, your businesses, your ministries. May your dreams and visions that have been revealed to you from God the Father come to fruition. May your basket always be filled with the provision of the Lord. May your hands prosper at every turn. May you grow old in grace and may God's favor continually surround you. All these things we pray in the spirit realm today for you – that your hearts and minds may be filled with the blessing and the joy of our Lord Jesus Christ. Let us stand together as one body of believers.

CHAPTER TWENTY-FIVE

PERSONAL MIRACLES

THIS CHAPTER IS an additional special chapter for all those who find themselves in a hard place especially in their financial and day-to-day situation, for all those going through a period of hardship, or on their way out of hardship.

The mental and physical stresses and pressures of life that come when one operates under severe financial pressures can hardly be explained to someone who has never experienced these challenges. The heart-breaking pressure of seeming continual lack and often of circumstances that in the natural seem to make no sense at all, can so often lead to us becoming heartsick and our faith getting hijacked.

When Rory and I were going through the very worst of times, there were so very, *very* few stories I could find where people had TRULY been in our position and come out on the other side. I remember clinging to the story about how Kenneth and Gloria Copeland had once sat on potato boxes (I think that's what they called them). Their experience gave me some hope because they too had once had nothing.

We were putting all the spiritual principles we knew into practice; we were trying our best to walk according to God's principles. We were fraught with human frailties but doing our best at the time. But nothing changed and circumstances stayed as brass.

Some of you, precious friends, may be out of God's will. But if you are, deep down in your heart you will know it. But I sense that there are very many others of you, who are actually IN the center of God's will, just in a preparational season and a season of refining before the great and memorable moment when the ignition key to your call is turned from Heaven itself and the Father Himself says – "Your Time Has Come."

Father, I pray for every man and every woman who walks at this time in a wilderness season of their life – and I ask for STRENGTH that they may see the season through. Today I ask for a supernatural confirmation of their FUTURE. That they may see Your great right hand move on their behalf. I ask that all those to whom You have poured out dreams and visions, that You confirm your call, that You CONFIRM Your hand upon their lives in a spectacular, INTIMATE way that today they know beyond any of the enemy's doubts that they are TRULY loved and adored by You and in the very palm of Your hand.

Father, I RELEASE TODAY men and women but especially MEN – I release the MEN – I release the HUSBANDS who have been bound by generational curses of FAILURE and I prophesy under the unction of the Most High God – that where you have failed in the past – so too that is the height of success in God that you have yet to experience in the future. We BREAK every yoke from the past – we break the curse of fatherlessness and low self-esteem. Father we CALL these men and women FORTH into DESTINY, DESTINY, DESTINY!

Says the Lord, "Come forth My Son – into Destiny. Come

forth, My Daughter, into the fullness of all I have prepared for you. For it is greater, far greater than all that is gone before. And Son – My Son – where you have seen failure at every turn – and where you have put your hand to the plow – and you have seen no seed come up out of the ground – and you have seen no vine bear fruit – so today I tell you – that in a just a little while – there shall be change. In just one more season," says the Lord – "RADICAL change shall fall upon your life. And the areas of weakness shall become great strength. And areas of depression shall turn to joy. And the dry and arid ground shall be watered. And the bare fields shall become fruitful. And the bare branch shall bud and the tree shall yield its fruit in season. And even as there have been those around you who have misunderstood the process, in years to come My plan shall be revealed. And great wonder shall arise. And great rejoicing shall come forth. For your life shall be as a garden in full blossom and you shall rejoice knowing that it is I, the Lord God of Israel, who has done this thing. So walk in My ways, My child. Take hold of My hand. And lift your face to Heaven and rejoice. For great and wondrous are the things in store for you. For I have not forsaken you. For I have not forgotten you. For your walls are ever before me. And My great Right Hand shall sustain you until that appointed time, when I shall lead you out of the wilderness, your head leaning upon My chest. And as one we shall walk. And as one we shall talk. And as one we shall minister. And YOU shall know that I am YOUR GOD who has led you out of the wilderness."

I'd like to just share a few miracles of encouragement especially for the ladies, concerning houses.

Houses are *so* important for us girls. Our men grow to understand this more as the years of marriage go on. But I believe with every fiber of my being, that a woman's desire for a home for her family is a GOD birthed desire from the very heart of God.

Yes – it all takes time; the processes of God are intertwined with the processes of earth and we have to mix faith and PATIENCE to receive the promises but I want to encourage you with my experiences in this area, and my desire is to share them today so that any of you who are feeling hopeless about *ever* living in a nice home may receive hope. Many of you reading this will already have homes of your own, but maybe God will stir you to add your faith to another dream that the Lord has placed inside your heart.

But for as many of you who have beautiful homes, there are thousands reading this who still continue to live in despair, for there is no way in the natural that you can see your desire could ever be met.

I remember so vividly when we lived in a flat above a shop in Hinchley Wood. Samantha, our eldest child, was a small baby. We were struggling terribly financially and I used to stare out longingly at the patch of green lawn in front of the shops in summer and pretend that it was my garden. From that point on, I dreamt about one day having a beautiful large green, lush English lawn! But it seemed IMPOSSIBLE!

The times in that flat were some of the deepest times of shame that Rory and I knew, when we were pouring into a vision that to all intents and purposes had no chance of becoming a reality, and there was no fruit, not even a tiny sprig showing about the ground. Everything that Rory touched failed – we had no money. No future. No hope. Except God.

During Rory's "music tour" deal period, things were starting to look better and for the first time money was coming in and we eventually managed to beg, borrow, scrimp, scrape enough together to purchase our very first small house as first time owners in East Molesey, England. It was a quaint, quirky, arty house and I *adored* it.

221

I was now expecting our second child, our son Christian, and now for the very first time, I would actually have my own house to bring my baby back to, as previously we had been in near bankruptcy in South Africa and Samantha was born in my mother-in-law's house. I had never had money to buy things for the babies without struggling (as many do today) and so this house really meant a lot to me.

Well, unfortunately, this was the hard preparational season of our life and also the time when the music deals fell apart (shortly after we moved in). We both lived day and night with the tremendous stresses of financial pressure. Most months we could hardly buy baby things, let alone pay the mortgage. Meanwhile God had spoken in this time about our call. But we still had to pay the bills!

To cut a long story short, after many months of grace from the mortgage lender, we finally launched the Channel on 1 October 1995, but the breakthrough had come too late to save our house. We LOST our first house in England at *exactly* the same time as we launched the Channel.

There is a process in Great Britain that once you lose a house, your name then goes onto a blacklist and you can't have your OWN mortgage again for SEVEN years!

Our name went on that list JUST as we launched Christian Channel Europe! I believe this is not as devastating for a man as it is for a woman, because basically unless he is a very unusual man – a MAN can live ANYWHERE – a TENT . . . a CARAVAN . . . a DESERT . . . but a woman longs for a HOME.

So now we had TWO babies and nowhere to live and had just started broadcasting across Europe! Well, we rented a place in Kent, then moved to Sunderland and stayed in a small room in a hotel until we got settled. And the FIRST miracle happened! We were visiting our lovely friends Ken and Lois Gott when, next door, we saw the house was up for sale. It was a lovely home. My heart sank, because I knew there was no way EVER to live in it. Well, after a long chain of miracles, God moved on a precious businessman and his wife's heart and they were SO KIND that they bought the house really just so we could live in it. It was such a breakthrough for us to have a stable beautiful home that I could decorate as though it was ours. God had moved in such a wonderful way.

Well, several years later, we started to look around for a property with a larger garden as the kids were past toddler stage and it would have been wonderful to have more space outside. We half-heartedly started looking. No joy. Then we felt led to earnestly ask the Lord. Well, we drove up a secluded drive in Sunderland and there facing us was this incredible old Manor House divided into three. It was like a *fairytale*.

Three huge Georgian windows looked out onto the most exquisite fairytale lawn you could dream of. There was a bench outside. Well, I sat down and I just COULDN'T leave. But it was IMPOSSIBLE in the natural! How could we *ever* afford to buy such a place? What a miracle was to occur!

Rory phoned, on the very outside off-chance, a South African businessman and treasured old friend. He is an incredibly generous man and a very canny and astute businessman, a deal maker! He had given a wonderful gift to the Channel during our London partner's evening from a forthcoming deal but, as often in any business deal, it had taken nearly a year for the actual deal to come through. That's business. So he said to Rory that he was involved in another deal. And IF it came through, *he* would personally buy the house especially FOR US and we could live in it!

What an incredible miracle – but our hopes seemed dashed in the natural as we HAD to give an answer to the house's owner and put the MONEY down in TWO WEEKS! What business deal is going to come through lock, stock and barrel in two weeks? And many other people also wanted the house.

223

But God's supreme hand moved.

In a matter of WEEKS the business deal was through in a supernatural time frame. The house was bought. The ONLY payment that this remarkable friend asked from us which was in our rental contract, was a rent of ONE RED ROSE ON A SUMMER'S DAY – once a year!

The incredible thing is that it was nearly winter when we moved in. And outside the three huge windows, budding alone – was ONE SOLITARY RED ROSE – A TOKEN OF THE Father's unending love and faithfulness to His children who couldn't get on their own property ladder!

The miracle doesn't stop there!

This amazing generous-hearted friend ALSO gave us money to pay off debts and he PAID for ALL the new carpets and curtains of my choice in this grand new home! I had never *never* experienced such an outpouring of financial blessing in my life.

When we gave this house up to settle in America, it was sold for exactly DOUBLE the price that he bought it for. God had doubled our precious friend's money. God blessed His servant's hand because he had blessed us without reserve!

Then yet another HOUSE miracle in America.

We lived in the "Box House" with minimal furniture for several months in Moravian Falls and then moved into Washington DC. Prices are exorbitant there! HOW would we EVER find anywhere??? To make things worse, we weren't eligible for ANY mortgage as we were on visa waivers at the time. And the MINISTRY wasn't eligible, as it had no asset base in America. We would have to rent AGAIN.

My heart sank. I was getting older, the kids were growing. We had moved from everything stable that we knew and had been living in someone else's house. I desperately wanted to decorate a house and make it a home. We had given up our most beautiful miracle home in

224

England – I couldn't face going back again to our early years of struggle.

Well – we drove through the beautiful historic town of Fredericksburg, Virginia and I caught my breath as we passed a house down the main street. It was a colonial house – JUST my taste. But there was no For Sale sign – in fact we couldn't see ANY For Sale signs ANYWHERE! Eventually in despair, we stopped at the local estate agents.

The VERY first house he showed us on his books was this house! By a miracle of God, some wonderful friends in the Assembly of God financial services assisted the ministry to buy the house as an investment. The ministry NOW had a property in America – the first asset on their books. It was a beautiful house. I decorated it with all my heart. The ministry sold it TWO YEARS later – for exactly DOUBLE its money AGAIN. Just when GOD TV most needed the cash! It was an incredible investment and blessing to us for the time to live in and as a financial investment for the ministry.

And here lies the latest HOUSE miracle. God is SO faithful!

I looked on the internet from America – at houses in England. Yes – we could rent AGAIN – but I had such a deep desire in my heart that this time when we came back to England, that for the first time since we had launched the Channel, that by some divine miracle this time we could get on the property ladder and this time could have our OWN house in England. I had been so happy to live in houses owned by other people, but it would be so NICE to finally own our *own* house in England.

But, once again, it would take a miracle as, although our name was now off the blacklist – because we had missed out all these years on the rising property ladder, we could in no way afford the huge deposits needed to be forthcoming on owning your own home as we had no house in the UK to sell and make a profit.

I scoured the internet. We had such a strong leading to the Plymouth area. But we had never even been there.

Eventually, there were two houses we saw. Both were impossible in the natural. One was sold immediately. The other we booked to look at on our scouting trip back from America.

Well, we drove off the main road and I nearly collapsed in wonder! We drove through hedgerows and tiny village lanes until we came to a tiny *tiny* village with just a Post Office, a shop and beautiful old Norman church.

What a place to write and worship. We had landed in the heart of the English countryside and we hadn't even known! Well, the house was an old English rectory. It was very unprepossessing from the outside as an unattractive sunroom extension masked the beautiful Georgian entrance.

But when we walked inside! It was almost an exact replica of the house we had left in Sunderland to go to America – except it seemed more a family home. It had old wooden floorboards, huge Georgian windows, one Victorian bathroom with views onto the country fields – and in front of it sprawled a beautiful large English lawn!

The house had already been on the market for almost a year and I was so thankful that the entrance to the main house was so unappealing as I'm convinced that the Lord kept it for us by its appearance.

Well – we had found the house – but how on EARTH could we get it? It was completely impossible!

Well, our amazing friend who had bought the wing of the Manor House on our behalf was set to sell some businesses and was happy to loan us the deposit. Meanwhile, we managed to arrange the rest of the mortgage. We arrived back in England and had been living from place to place out of suitcases. We had flown from New York to Tel Aviv, broadcast live from Israel, then arrived in England, come down to Plymouth, pushing forward our new GOD TV premises, then traveled back up to Sunderland for Mission's Week. Our life consisted of miles of traveling.

Back to the West Country, settling the children in school, then back to Dorset seeing Daddy who was so very frail by this time, then visiting dogs the OTHER end of Devon in quarantine, then conducting business in London, then back to Dorset, then setting things up in Plymouth. Finally we managed to find a rented place for two weeks, then we had to move again.

We were now exhausted. We had lived out of suitcases non-stop for nearly nine weeks. The completion date for the closure on the house was just over a week away. We were so very excited. Then the bombshell came. Our dear friend had been through a devastating and tragic divorce. THE VERY DAY THE DEPOSIT for our house was to be transferred, his spouse froze all his assets through a High Court injunction. *THE VERY DAY*.

I was devastated. We were exhausted from living out of suitcases and moving from pillar to post. There was absolutely NO way we could get our hands on the amount of money needed for the deposit. It was a complete impossibility.

I know that many of you, who are not in ministry, may think – it's all right for you in ministry – there's **always** someone to help those who are in ministry. But please let me add here, that after many conversations with ministry friends, that, dear one, is simply NOT the truth.

It seems to be a RARE thing in ministry that any of us in ministry actually receives extra blessings. The truth is that we live just like everyone else and a miracle for us is of just as great a magnitude as for anyone out there who is not in ministry.

That is what makes all of these miracles even greater for us and how much we are awed that they are from the Lord's hand.

Time was running out. In the natural it now looked like we would LOSE the house and now be stranded in England having come back in faith. There was nowhere to settle – we had to start searching from scratch.

I wish I could tell you that I was a remarkable figure of faith, standing stalwart and strong, never flinching. But the opposite is true. And I PROMISED my wonderful heavenly Father through all this that I would SHARE with you HONESTLY what happened so that you too would know His great and tender mercies extend to our lapses in behavior!! Oh, He is so incredible.

Well, I collapsed inside. It was as though all the early years of hardship and struggle came back to taunt me. The devil said, you see – You'll NEVER have a home. You're going to have to live in a rented flat for years until you get established! I sat next to my poor sick earthly father, who prayed for me.

I couldn't eat. I could hardly sleep. I felt like I had ZERO faith. Our wonderful amazing intercessors in Scotland continued to fervently push through for us.

I was a total liability in the faith camp! Just crying out to the Lord for His mercy! I had stood for eleven years through hell and high water, and now, in one fell swoop ... I was a gibbering wreck! I remember saying to the Lord – "I'm too old to go through this ..." I whimpered pitifully, "... I'm almost approaching menopause ..." I continued. As though my pre-menopausal ramblings were going to radically move the Father's hand on my behalf!

"I have to write *Messiah* ..." I continued ...

"I have to launch the Channel for America ..." My voice trailed off.

But you see, there are times when our wonderful heavenly Father needs us to know that it is not on OUR faith alone, it is NOT because of OUR works, it is not on OUR perfection – but that it rests on HIS LOVE. It's about Him and HIS FAITHFULNESS, HIS

MERCIES, HIS GREAT AND INFINITELY TENDER COMPASSIONS. Even as our own earthly fathers bless us because they LOVE us, so our heavenly Father, who understands that we are made of dust, He Himself gathers us as we cry and feebly flail around in our own weakness and holds us to His breast and whispers "Peace. Peace, My Child." And He calms the raging seas.

And that is what my wonderful heavenly Father did for me. And I promised Him I would tell you the truth, that you too could have hope in His incredible and unfailing love.

And so it was, that in a matter of days, when all looked completely lost – when all hopes of buying the house seemed gone that the Lord moved in a mighty way – and that our indomitable and wonderful Mr X (who will recognize himself from this!) arranged a loan for the deposit on the house. We believe we are in the midst of a miracle on this and will update you as the months go past!

Today, I am sitting writing this book in my home office surrounded by glorious English fields, cows and sheep, in the very house that I saw all those months ago on the internet while still in Fredericksburg.

Oh – our incredible heavenly Father will never fail us.

He is the most wonderful Father in Heaven and on earth.

His love will never fail you.

His tender mercies and compassions are always reaching out to you.

Even if you are in the most awful place today, where all hope seems gone and your dreams are shattered. He is not a man that He should desert us in our weakest times. He is the mighty God of Israel. The God who knows.

The God who sees.

The God who hears the very whisper of your heart. The God who acts. The God who loves.

"For as the heavens are high above the earth, so great are His mercy and loving-kindness toward those who reverently and worshipfully fear Him.

As far as the east is from the west, so far has He removed our transgressions from us.

As a father loves and pities his children, so the Lord loves and pities those who fear Him – with reverence, worship, and awe.

For He knows our frame; He [earnestly] remembers and imprints [on His heart] that we are dust."

(Psalm 103:11–14 AMP)

As it is written in Psalm 97:

"The LORD reigns, let the earth rejoice;
Let the many islands be glad.
Clouds and thick darkness surround Him;
Righteousness and justice are the foundation of His throne.
Fire goes before Him
And burns up His adversaries round about.
His lightnings lit up the world;
The earth saw and trembled."

(Psalm 97:1–4 NASB)

And yet, this same incredible wondrous Almighty God, before whom we fall prostrate and fling our faces to the ground in awe and trembling, this same Almighty God – is He who has chosen us for fellowship with Him.

He has chosen us out of the whole of Heaven and earth as His beloved – to hold to His breast as His dearly beloved children, to live within His glorious and tender presence for all eternity.

What inconceivable love is this?

Our Glorious Father who has taken us up from our conception.

Who has nurtured us by day and covered us by night in our mother's womb.

Who Himself has taken us up even in times when we were rejected by all men.

He *alone* is our Father.

He is our mighty redeemer.

He who sent His Son to redeem us.

Because He loved us so passionately.

Oh – for the Father Himself could not bear to be without us. He could not bear to be without YOU. And He tenderly, oh so tenderly loves you.

And He will never *never ever* fail *YOU.*

Note: From Rory and Wendy

And so – today we stand at the brink of a new era, a new season for GOD TV. On 1 October 2006, our eleventh birthday, the signal of GOD TV beamed across North America from our brand new broadcast center and studios at the base of Mount Zion in the center of Jerusalem. From New York to Los Angeles.

We have such a Holy Spirit excitement in our spirits. We are so excited about the future for GOD TV, and so excited at the prospect that millions of Americans from all across North America join with our GOD TV family in Great Britain, in Europe, in India, in Hong Kong, across the nations of Africa, Australia, New Zealand and beyond, to stand together as a corporate body of believers. To pray. To worship. To war. That the purposes of Almighty God may be done.

There are so many amazing things in the pipeline for GOD TV as we launch into the Americas and as our hearts continue to burn for the evangelization of the Far East including communist China – but that will take another book. To date, GOD TV broadcasts to over 122 million television households to over 438 million viewers across 216 nations.

ALL glory to the Father of our Lord Jesus Christ.

In the meantime, this is our prayer for GOD TV and all our viewers around the world...

May the Father's Kingdom come here on Earth as it is in
    Heaven.
May His Kingdom be established across the globe and may
    GOD TV long continue to be a part of this process. Firstly
    in Europe, then in the Middle East, and from Israel into
    Africa and Asia, from Jerusalem to the ends of the earth,
    may the Church be equipped and countless souls saved.
May all God's dreams for you come to pass.
May His destiny for you never be thwarted.
May you follow His voice each day of your lives, no matter
    where He leads you.
May His will be done in your lives as we all stand on the brink
    of the greatest end-time move ever to sweep across the
    face of the earth. To all our viewers in India, Africa, Hong
    Kong, Europe and Australia, you are such a part of this
    next move.
We love you, America. We love you, Great Britain.
We are here to serve you, America. We are here to serve you,
    Great Britain.
We *shall* see revival in North America and Great Britain and it
    shall be a flame that will affect the entire world.
You are part of our family. You live in our hearts.
With all our love always.

Rory and Wendy Alec

PROPHETIC WORDS FOR AMERICA

AMERICA – THE DAY AND THE HOUR OF REVIVAL APPROACHES

"I have heard the cries of those that hunger – of those that have fallen on their faces before Me, seeking, imploring Me for a move of My Presence. For an outpouring of My Person and of My Presence across the shores of America – and I tell you this day – that this hour dawns upon your shores."

"That the wind of My Presence is stirring – That those who have longed to see this day shall yet see this move in their generation – For where sin abounds – surely my grace abounds more abundantly."

"And because of the prayers of My saints in this nation," says the Lord God of Hosts – *"because of the fervent prayers and the supplications of a remnant in this nation – so my hand shall move across the United States of America for the great outpouring of My Holy Spirit that has yet to fall."*

"And so, beloved, I tell you that My presence shall fall from East to West from North to South – and Canada – yes surely Canada shall be a part of this revival," says the Lord of Hosts – *"and yes – I have heard the cries of My people – I have seen the repentance of the*

hearts of those of My people who have not let Me go day or night – and so I tell you this day that the prayers of the intercessors of this nation – the declarations of the prophets of this nation – have rent the heavens and have risen up before My throne like a sweet incense – an incense that burns fervently before My throne both day and night – And so My children I am coming to this nation – oh My children, I come quickly to this nation."

I Am Calling My Apostles, My Prophetic Evangelists

"And now I would address the apostles – Rise, Rise, Rise up in the nation of America – Apostles – for surely the intercessions and the supplications of the saints have prepared the way for your feet to march and for your hands to build – and the prophets, the voices of My prophets have rent the heavens and now, apostles, it is time for you to rise and build – to break open the gates of brass and the doors of iron – for in this time and in this season – oh yes – a new anointing shall fall upon My apostles in this hour in America – and the gates that were brass shall open and the doors that were iron shall swing forth."

"Oh yes, and some would say, 'but we have seen the new move' – Oh no, no," says the Lord – "there is coming a new day and yet a new hour that has not been seen yet upon the earth – And now I call you evangelists – for such a time you have been birthed for in America – and yes, there have been those who have plowed the fields that are white unto harvest – white unto harvest – but there is a new breed of evangelist that rises upon your shores, America – and it is you whom I call forth – for surely although you have seen harvest – the harvest you have reaped has been but a glimmer of what I have birthed in your spirit – I tell you that even in a moment it shall be – even in a moment – that My breath shall blow and like a whirlwind – a different season and a different dispensation shall fall."

235

"And I shall raise up My prophetic evangelists and as they declare – and as they bring forth – so I tell you that My consuming fire shall fall – and there shall be a holy fear – a holy dread of Me that shall sweep this nation – America – and thousands times thousands times thousands shall fall to their knees in repentance as My consuming fire starts to sweep across halls, across arenas, across stadiums – for America stands on the outskirts of revival – but make no mistake for it is nothing that has gone before – but it is everything that the generals of old saw in the spirit realm and longed to see in their day – and so I shall raise up a mighty generation."

The Consuming Fire of My Presence Shall Roar Across the Youth of America

"And many, many, many, yes many of them, shall be the youth of this nation – for I tell you – there is coming a fire – the consuming fire of My presence that will roar across the YOUTH of the nation of America and consume the lukewarmness and the dross and the things of the world shall be consumed in its wake and a great move of repentance shall fall across the youth of this nation. The YOUTH," says the Lord – *"the YOUTH of AMERICA – And as the tears of repentance fall and as the youth of this nation fall prostrate on their face – so My mighty Generals and Apostles shall join across America in a great and fearsome army of the Lord – And it shall be a new sound – and it shall be a new wind from heaven – the wind shall roar through the highways and byways of America – it is the sound of marching – marching – to the step and the sound of the Lord of Hosts – and the sleeping Church shall awaken – and Prophets – My Prophets – I call you – rise up in this day and in this hour and cry out, cry out to America – for the time to demolish the religious strongholds that have bound My people so tightly in their fetters – it is the season and the hour for the bonds of brass to be broken, for the*

shackles of iron to be shattered by the declarations of My Prophets –
For My Church has been in a slumber – for My Church has been in a
stupor – but this is coming, My season for America – And there will
be food for the hungry" – says the Lord – *"there will be food for the*
hungry in spirit – there will be sustenance and nourishment – and
the eagles that lie weak and dying – many, many, many of those who
should be strongest in this hour have fallen from the skies through
lack of sustenance and I am moved with compassion for My eagles in
this hour – and I am moved with compassion upon the young eagles
of this nation who are starving – and so I will feed America with that
which is straight from My hand – with a word from heaven – with
sustenance that will sustain them through the coming days."

America – A Shift Ahead – A Great Sifting

"For I tell you America, – that the times and the seasons are
changing – and a time of persecution dawns – a time when agendas
will rise to the surface – for there comes a shift ahead – a shift in the
political arenas in the years ahead – and a great sifting of believers
in America will take place – but out of this sifting My remnant shall
rise – pure and true – with a clear voice – and a clarion call – but the
cost is dear – for the cost is everything – For I tell you that the time
will come in America when it is no longer politically correct to be
called 'Christian' and many, many, many of My children shall fall
away in that day and that hour – but for all who are founded on the
rock – for all who hear and hearken to the voice of My Spirit – they
shall know that in that day and in that hour – I shall come with My
mighty right hand to save them when the great times of persecution
have begun – I am coming soon."

"For I am calling for relationship not lip-service – I am calling
My Church in America higher, higher, higher – higher into a
relationship with My Person and My Presence – I am calling My

Church, America, out from the religious bondage and trappings of her past – and I will use my remnant to cry out – and the Church shall turn – and the sleeping Church shall rise from its slumber in the times of persecution ahead – And I shall light a TORCH – a TORCH – a literal TORCH of the fire of My Saints of America – a torch that shall set ablaze the world – for it is time to look OUT, America – beyond your cities beyond your towns – Look out, Look OUT, America – for the nations have need of you – Rise up from the bondage of complacency – for the East cries out to you – and the North travails – and the South calls to you in the Spirit – and so My fire shall fall – and from the East Coast to the West and from the West across the seas it shall go – and from the North it shall rise North, North even to Russia – it shall burn – and to the South – the South a flame of fire shall rise."

I Shall Do a New Thing in the Bible Belt

"And the Bible Belt that has kept My Word – and has revered My Name – I shall do a NEW THING IN THE BIBLE BELT – for there is yet a new move that shall spring forth – for children – your present sustenance cannot sustain you in the days ahead," says the Lord – "and I will break the bounds of your establishment – and I shall come towards you in this day, yet in a new form – and yes many, many, many in the new day shall not recognize Me – they shall say, 'Oh, this is not God' – but I shall pour out such a spirit of hunger of hunger, of hunger upon you – that your desperation for Me shall overcome your religious expectation.

"Oh yes – and a new breath of My Spirit shall wash over you – and fresh and living waters shall flow upon you – and you shall drink of My Presence and you shall drink of My fire and the eyes of your spirit shall be opened – and I tell you that like a tree set ablaze so the Bible Belt shall come into a new realm and a new fresh move in Me –

and shall be fed – and shall join with the great and mighty dread
army of the Lord as she rises across America – America, America –
Beloved America. And then the Judgment will FALL."

"But My Church shall BLAZE with My glory."

VISION OF THE EAGLES ACROSS AMERICA

And in this vision I saw hundreds of thousands, maybe millions of
baby eagles, that were amassed all within the shape of the continent
of North America. Most of them were young infant eagles, and they
were weakened and scrawny, their feathers did not grow, and many of
them had no feathers at all.

They looked bald. As I watched, they were screeching and crying
out and the Lord said to me – "They are starving. They have not been
fed. They have little sustenance."

I raised my eyes to the skies overhead and I saw many, many
huge full-grown eagles. And they should have been so beautiful. So
noble. So strong. I sensed that they were golden eagles. And then I
grew extremely distressed. For the older, full-grown eagles started to
hurtle and fall from the skies, it seemed through sheer weakness and
lack of food.

And the Lord said, *"It is not only My babes who are starving –*
Many, many, many of My generals and My leaders are still eating
that which cannot sustain them in the coming days and when the
pressure becomes intense they fall from the sky because they have
become so weak." And I could see that this was a terribly distressing
thing for the Lord to watch – for I could see how desperately He loved
these eagles, as they loved Him and had tried to follow Him to the
best of their ability.

Then the Lord showed me smaller camps dotted across North
America.

Many of these were prophetic streams of the day. They were the Cavalry – the ground troops preparing for war. And here the eagles were strong and healthy and their feathers were gleaming.

The babies were strutting and well nourished and ready to fly. But then the Lord showed me that each of these camps, although they had food that was essential for survival and the food was reaching their cities and their communities, I saw that the food was being hijacked further along the way as it moved out from their apostolic covering and was in very many instances not stretching further than their own territories in which they lived.

And then the Lord said to me – *"I have placed a mantle upon GOD TV in this day and in this hour for America that GOD TV's voice will be one that shall reach across the continent and will AMPLIFY, AMPLIFY these messages, this sustenance – that the scrawny dying eagles shall hear and regain hope and strength. That the large dying golden eagles' strength shall be renewed and they shall feed once more and be nourished."*

And then I saw that as the Father Himself used GOD TV as one of His tools to bring these streams together and AMPLIFY the message of sustenance for these times – The scrawny baby eagles grew strong and prepared to fly. The weakened golden eagles were healed and strengthened and in turn fed their flocks of baby eagles. Then I saw, throughout America, a Great Army of strong noble eagles rise up and fly to take the Gospel to the ends of the earth before the Second Coming of Our Lord Jesus Christ.

And the armies on the ground were covered by the Airforce and the Airforce was covered by the armies on the ground.

And it was strategic and all the streams were divinely aligned.

And the Prophets marched ahead, the Sword of the Spirit in their hands, and the prophetic intercessors took up the rear.

I saw the great generals and apostles of the day leading their great armies – All walking to a divine rhythm – a sovereign timeline from heaven. And the pastors and the teachers were in the great camps where the warriors were gathered.

And the teachers, now baptized in a new and a fresh prophetic anointing, were teaching the eagles, preparing them for warfare and imparting strategy. And the pastors had such Father's hearts – and a great mentoring and discipling was taking place.

And the Lord said – "In this new move – there is NO ONE left BEHIND." And I could see that even the very young and the very, very old were being pastored and nurtured and cared for. And this seemed very pleasing to the Lord.

And the pastors were so consumed with caring for the people that there was no covetousness, no territorialism and this also seemed pleasing and good to the Lord. And I could glimpse the prophets ahead and their faces were like flint. And their eyes flashed with the fierceness of their Holy God.

And it seemed as if they were marching before the apostles – their cries and declarations making a path for the great generals and apostles who followed after them with their fearsome armies of the Lord. And it was strategic. And it was divinely aligned. And was orchestrated not by one but by each in his own correctly aligned position. And the Lord said – *"Position! Position! It is high time and the season for My Church to know their position – and become divinely aligned, that the greatest and the least serves in my preordained place in My Kingdom."* This was of vital importance to the Lord in these times.

And as the great armies marched forward, so the stragglers and the backslidden and the lukewarm ventured out to watch them. And the warriors were calling "Come, join us!" And the spirit was so strong, that immediately the backsliders came into the proximity of the army, they fell to their knees in repentance and were taken off to the camps where the pastors and the teachers cleaned them and fed them until they were strong enough to join. And millions, yes, millions of those who had previously been left behind, became great warriors for the Last Days.

PROPHECY AFTER 7th JULY BOMBINGS IN LONDON

I saw several pockets of small fires across Europe – the fires of wicked men and organizations – and the Lord said *"Holland"* – Holland was very strong – then France – and then Spain and Italy – then the Lord said – *"And to the North"* – it was very clear and the Holy Spirit's voice was insistent and very strong – *"The NORTH – the North – the North."* And I had no clear understanding at all what the Lord meant and then I sensed a circle and heard the Holy Spirit say – *"North London – Northern England – Northern Europe."* And then I heard *"North Africa"* – this was the circle and the circle seemed to me to be linked in some way.

These fires, God said, were kindling fires – they were very small – hardly noticeable on the map – but they burned furiously – and had fiercely burning blue flames – and then I saw that some kind of NET was being loosed from the heavenlies down to earth – and I heard the Lord say – *"THIS IS THE SNARE OF HEAVEN"* – and I saw a great angelic host – the warring host of Heaven being dispatched across Great Britain and Europe and other Northern-most and Middle-Eastern parts of the earth with swords that glistened like flaming fires – And the Lord said – *"As in the ancient of times – so as My people humble themselves and pray – a great and mighty roar of battle shall be unleashed from the heavenlies – and My mighty warring angels shall go forth – for I shall send them from the North and from the South."* God was saying these were the fires of wicked men and organizations across Great Britain and Europe and beyond.

Then I saw prayer start to rise – first from small pockets of intercessors across the British Isles – these were not just prayer movements and organizations – but they were the heartfelt prayers of the saints from towns and villages all across Great Britain – these were the praying mothers and grandmothers and grandfathers – these were the prayers of the intercessors across Great Britain – and yes – they were mostly women in their homes and in tiny prayer and home groups – fallen on their knees and on their faces – and I could see that they had the full attention of the Lord – and then I saw the men – and the men were the ministers of God – and the pastors and the ministers from all across Britain rose and joined their prayers in the Spirit with the prayers of the handmaidens – and the prophets started to prophesy – and join with the apostles and the intercessors – and then they were joined by the praying saints from across pockets in Europe and then from the North, East, South and West – and I saw a great hand arise from the North and the South and the East and the West – And the Lord said *"Because of the heartfelt prayers of My saints – I shall send My Angelic Host and the sound of their battle cry shall resound through the four corners of the earth as they prepare to meet the Princes of Darkness – For I tell you, My children – A great and terrible darkness has been unleashed upon the earth in these days – BUT I am raising up an army – I am raising up a mighty army of My people who will gird themselves up for battle – and as the sound of their voices rises up to me – and as the sound of their prayers – of their supplications comes before My throne – so in turn – My mighty warring angels be unleashed to do battle in the heavenlies."*

"And through the prayers of My saints in Great Britain – through the prayers of My saints in Great Britain – through the prayers of the saints and My followers in Great Britain – the stupor and the slumber and the secular humanistic spirits that have bound My people in this nation shall start to uproot – for my Church has had an outward semblance of power – yet its sound has been a whisper – even as My children have raised their voice in the streets of

Great Britain – so the spirits of secularism and humanism have bound the mouths of My saints – but I tell you, My children – there dawns another day" – says the Lord – *"there dawns a different hour – and I call you, Oh Church – I call you My saints – This is the day and this is the hour to arise"* – says the Lord – *"This is the hour to stir yourselves even as the mighty men of old – lift your voices and your hearts up to My throne – for this is the day and the hour of supplication."*

Then as the saints rose and started to pray – not with lip service but fervent heartfelt prayer from the heart – I saw another fire – with fierce white and orange living flames – start to burn – the prayers of the Church in Britain – and although it too started in pockets – this was the most incredible fire in the way that it spread across the nation – It was so fierce that as it took on power – it seemed that nothing could stop its path – but the people who created the fire were fallen on their knees – and God said *"Penitent hearts"* – and I knew somehow that these praying saints were repenting on behalf of Britain for the sins of the nation and for the sins of omission of the Church in Great Britain.

And these prayers gave the angels much strength – and the Snare of the Lord fell like a net across the dark hidden places of the earth – and I saw the terrifying whirlwind of the Lord like a fierce black whirlwind literally chase some of the evil blue pockets down – the winnowing whirlwind of the Lord of Hosts.

Then the Lord showed me a large lion – and He said – *"This lion represents the nation of Great Britain"* – And it was a shocking sight – for where the lion should have been filled out and sleek and gleaming – it was almost a skeleton – and its mane was barely visible – and its coat was covered in mange – and its roar which should have shaken the nations in its power and in its ferocity was strangled and barely audible. And the Lord said *"This represents both the glory of this nation at present and the state of My Church as a whole in Great*

Britain." And I saw in great letters – the words – "THE GLORY HAS DEPARTED FROM THE LION – BUT THE GLORY OF THE LORD OF HOSTS SHALL RETURN AND THE LION SHALL ROAR AGAIN."

And the Lord said – *"Bring back My glory – Bring back My glory that your nation may once more walk in the glory of its destiny – and the Church may show forth My glory"* – And the Lord showed me a huge flourishing green tree that was planted in the European mainland – its huge trunk seemed to be planted in Brussels and the foliage had grown so dense that the trees branches and foliage had grown over the English channel and covered Britain in a great dark shadow and thousands of smaller offshoots and branches had taken deep root in Great Britain – and I saw the roots tangled and grown into London and then through the British Isles up all the way to Scotland.

The Lord said – *"These are the deep roots of secularism and humanism that have taken deep root in this nation – these are the roots that are eroding this nation's faith!"* And I saw thousands upon thousands of people bowing in obedience to this tree and the roots were tightly twisted around their ankles – but they seemed totally unaware of this – that they were bound – and so they rejected the faith of their fathers – and I saw a great scoffing and a great decline in the traditions and the foundations of the past – and this mass of people was divided into two camps – the first huge mass of people whose ankles were bound by the gnarling roots of the green tree from Europe were younger and seemed more modern in their approach – and I saw written over their head – "UNBELIEF" – "CYNICISM" – "HUMANISM" – and the foliage and green leaves seemed to shadow their heads – and I sensed that they were being attacked at a cerebral level.

But the second group seemed to be those whose roots and foundations were from the established traditional denominations of Britain – yet they were just as affected as this first group – but I saw written over their head – "PRIDE" – "SKEPTICISM" – "CLOSED MINDEDNESS" – and I sensed that the roots around their ankles had bound them in a different manner – that even if they heard the call of the Spirit in these days that the spiritual forces had them so bound that they could not move with the tide and the times of God – and I saw the green foliage literally cover and shadow their foreheads and eyes and I saw the word "BLINDING."

And I said to the Lord, "Father – what does this mean?" And He said – *"The spirits that led Europe into post-Christian decline – have invaded Great Britain over these past decades – and have infiltrated and overshadowed the nation with the same humanism and paganism and secularism – and yet Britain is still so blinded by her roots and her foundations that she is still declaring herself a Christian nation"* – but the Lord says – *"That she has been shackled by the enemy."* And I said, "Lord what can break the shackles?"

And the Lord spoke and said, *"The prayers and fervent supplications of My saints in Great Britain – the repentance for the sins of commission and omission on behalf of the governments of Great Britain – on behalf of the people of Great Britain."* Then I asked the Lord about the Church – and He showed me thousands of people all belonging to different denominations with divisions and literally multitudes of OPINIONS – and somehow it seemed that the people's opinion was all more important in their eyes than God's opinion and I heard Him say: *"Until their opinions become My opinion the Church will continue to be divided among itself and be weak and underfed and lack the true POWER of GOD – Oh yes,"* says the Lord – *"There are many meetings – there are many committees – there are many opinions – opinions – but it is not the opinion and the thoughts of men's hearts that will change the destiny of Great Britain – but the opinion and the thoughts and intents of the word of the Living God – Humble yourselves – Humble yourselves and put aside your opinions and press into me the Living God for a living Word"* – And the Lord said – *"A humble and penitent heart I will not despise"* – and I saw the words written – "DIVISIONS AND FACTIONS."

Then as people dropped to their knees all over Britain from every walk of life and denomination the lion started to change – and He grew strong and sleek and his roar grew stronger. And I saw written in the spirit – "Create in me a clean heart, O God – and renew a right spirit within me." And as the people started to seek the face of the Lord I saw the word "COURAGE" – and I knew that in the spirit realm Great Britain had been endowed from the beginning of time with the mantle "COURAGE" – and the Lord said "LIONHEART."

And God said Britain has yet to move into her end-time destiny in the nations – And I saw again in great letters – the words – "THE GLORY HAS DEPARTED FROM THE LION – BUT THE GLORY OF THE LORD OF HOSTS SHALL RETURN." And the lion's roar by now had gained strength.

And then the Lord said – *"Manchester – Newcastle – then Birmingham – London – Edinburgh – Glasgow – Southampton – Bournemouth."* And I heard Him say *"Airports"* – not airlines but airports – *"Malls – shopping centers"* – that He was urging the saints to pray a higher protection over these places and over these things – and I felt Him go back once again to around Manchester – again I do not understand why. And then He started to speak of Great Britain's destiny...

SECOND PROPHECY

"O Great Britain, Great Britain – Isle of walls and of fortresses – I tell you that even as the glory of the Lord has departed from the Lion – so the glory of the Lion of Judah shall return – and My glory shall rest upon the Lion and the Lion once again shall open its mouth and its roar shall be heard again among the nations of this earth."

"For even, as in times past, the Lion whelped many, many cubs and sent its missionaries even to the uttermost parts of the earth, so I

tell you that the glory of these latter days shall be greater than that of the former – and even though in centuries past – so I sent missionaries out from this nation even to Africa, to India, to China and beyond – so I tell you, beloved, that in the decades to come, a great mobilizing of My called out ones shall occur – of men and women and boys and girls from these shores – those who even slumber at this time shall start to arise," says the Lord.

I Am About to Blow the Trumpet

"For even as many of My children – even as much of My Church in Great Britain slumbers even this day – so I declare that I am about to blow the trumpet," says the Lord, *"Yes, I the Lord God of Hosts, am about to blow the trumpet in Zion – and it shall resound with a mighty roar from the heavens – and My glory shall start to fall – and My Church and My called out ones shall rouse themselves from their stupor and from their slumber,"* says the Lord.

"For even now – I have heard the prayers of My people – Even now – although it be but a remnant – I have heard the prayers of the watchmen on the walls of Great Britain – the watchmen who neither slumber nor sleep – and even as they have cried out to me in the midnight hour for Britain to heed My voice and to seek My face – so I tell you, My children, that the day of the Lord is appearing. And they shall rise from the East and from the West of this Isle – they shall rise from the Southernmost tip to the North – and Scotland – yes Scotland," says the Lord.

"Yes – My burning fire shall be ignited in the furthermost parts of the North – and My glory shall light a flame," says the Lord, *"that shall sweep across divides and denominations – and the Pentecostals and the Evangelicals and the Anglicans, the Methodists, the Catholics and all who revere My name and the sacrifice of My Son shall unite with one heart and as one body – and that flame shall*

248

be seen across this land – and the cities and the villages of this nation shall start to burn with the fervency and the hunger of the Living God. For even as My Church has been bound by the shackles of compromise and passivity – I tell you that in this coming day and in this coming hour – My firebrands shall start to rise."

Like Wilberforce, My Apostolic Voices Shall Rise in the Houses of Parliament

"And like Wilberforce – My apostolic voices shall rise in the Houses of Parliament – they shall arise in London – they shall arise in Edinburgh – they shall arise in the North of England – and even as the unions had a voice in past years that was strident and rose above the crowds and became the voice of the masses – so in like manner shall My Church's voice start to be heard in a manner far above and beyond these present days."

"And so I shall raise My apostles – and they shall stand at the city gates and the gates of trading – and they shall stand in the government – and they shall stand in the media – and in the banking institutions and in businesses – and they shall stand in the clergy of this nation. And I shall raise up My prophets – and they shall rise – and their faces will be as flint – and even as John Knox's voice rang out above Scotland – I tell you that My prophets' voices shall start to rise in this nation – and I call My intercessors – I call My intercessors – Pray, Pray – do not desist from your prayers – for even that which you have perceived in your spirits and that which you have yearned for – it is almost upon you."

A Mighty Flood of Evangelists

"For surely the day of the missionaries dawns once more upon these shores – For surely the day of the Gospel going forth to the uttermost parts of the earth dawns once more upon these shores. And as My fire starts to fall across Great Britain – I tell you that the men, the women, boys and girls – shall feel the call to leave theses isles and to travel to the continents of the earth to preach My Gospel – And a mighty flood of evangelists – a mighty throng of missionaries shall leave this nation – and I shall thrust them into the four corners of the earth – and they shall go to Japan – and they shall go to Beijing – and they shall go to Africa – East and West – and they shall go to Europe – and to the Middle East – and I shall spread them as a net over the continent of Asia."

"And I shall open doors to My Gospel that have previously been shut – Even the doors of iron and of brass shall be opened unto the missionaries from the British Isles – Vietnam – North Korea and beyond. And there shall be a great flood and a torrent of My Gospel that shall once more go forth from this land – And I shall send Bibles from this land – and I shall send resources – resources – resources from Great Britain – that will feed – that will clothe – that will build – that will teach – that will establish My Gospel in the four corners of the earth. For this is the destiny of this land in latter days," says the Lord – "To resource – to nurture – to establish – to preach My Gospel. And even as in past days – this Empire was established – so I tell you that in this coming day and this coming hour it shall be the Empire of the Great King of Heaven that shall be established."

The Rise of One in Great Britain with a Rod of Iron and My Government Upon His Shoulders

"And there has yet to rise from these shores one who has a rod of iron – in the decades to come – you shall yet see one rise who has My government upon his shoulders – and he shall rise in the govern- ment – and he shall rise in this nation and he shall rule with a rod of iron," says the Lord. *"And he will come at such a time when Great Britain is faltering – and I shall do this because of the prayers of My people – For there shall be a great swarm that shall rise against these isles in the decades to come – A great swarm as an army will arise across the waters around this nation – but this man with the rod of iron shall stand firm – And the nation shall take courage – and the lionheart of Britain shall arise as one – and the great swarm shall turn back and even in an instant – be stopped in their tracks,"* says the Lord.

The Great Joining of the Lion and the Eagle

"And there will be a great joining of the Lion and the Eagle – For even as the Eagle came to the Lion's aid in times gone by – so I tell you that in this coming season – once again this alliance between the Lion and the Eagle shall be forged and the forge shall not be broken," says the Lord, – *"because it is destined by Heaven.*

"And a great wave of prayer shall rise up from the East Coast of America through the heartland to the West – and that wave of prayer and intercession shall wash across Britain as a fiercely burning flame – and shall cleanse and protect – but in the years ahead – so the prayers of the saints in Britain shall rise and like a wave they shall spread across America – and preserve and protect – and a great joining shall occur and this joining shall not be the joining of man," says the Lord *"but the joining of Almighty God."*

"And this nation shall return to its Christian roots – It shall RETURN to its Christian roots – and the glory of the Lion of Judah shall once more return and rest upon the Lion."

"IF my people repent of the sins of this nation and humble themselves and pray."

OTHER BOOKS BY WENDY ALEC

Journal of the Unknown Prophet

Wendy Alec's powerful book is a divine revelation of the Lord Jesus
Christ and His cry for a deeper intimacy with each and every person
on earth.

For the unbeliever, it represents a profound picture of who Jesus
really is and how much He cares – how He has always been there
for them, and how He wants to enrich their lives. For the believer,
it is an extraordinary challenge to walk in the fullness of everything
God has in store for His beloved children.

Read or listen to excerpts at www.unknownprophet.com

Journal of the Unknown Prophet is available from GOD TV for
$18 per copy excluding postage and packing. To order please call
your GOD TV regional office.

CONTACTS

For more information about ministry of Rory & Wendy Alec or how you can watch the GOD Channel in your area, please log on to www.god.tv or contact your GOD TV regional office (see below).

E-mails to Rory & Wendy can be sent to roryandwendy@god.tv

AFRICA

South Africa
GOD TV Africa
PO Box 79, Milnerton, Cape Town, 7435, South Africa
Telephone: +27 (0) 21 555–1206
E-mail: info.africa@god.tv

Nigeria
GOD TV West Africa
34 Old Aba Road, Rumuogba, PO Box 6477, Port Hartcourt, Nigeria
E-mail: info.africa@god.tv

AMERICA

Florida, USA
GOD TV North America
405 Douglas Ave Suite 1555, Altamonte Springs, Florida 32714
Telephone: 001 407 862 5084
E-mail: info.usa@god.tv

GOD TV Central Office:
Suite 905, 1730 M Street, NW, Washington DC, 20036, USA
Telephone: 001 202 223 4023

AUSTRALIA/OCEANIA

Australia
GOD TV Australasia
PO Box 697, Liverpool, NSW 2170 Australia
Telephone: 1 300 368 311
E-mail: info.australia@god.tv/info.newzealand@god.tv

EUROPE

England
GOD TV UK & Ireland
PO Box 1500, Sunderland SR1 1WP, Tyne & Wear, UK
Telephone: +44 (0) 870 60 70 446
E-mail: info@god.tv

Germany
GOD TV Europe
Valentinskamp 24, 20354, Hamburg, Germany
Telephone: +49 (0) 40 414 317 314
E-mail: info.europe@god.tv

Denmark
GOD TV Scandinavia
PO Box 12, DK 9800, Hjorring, Denmark
Telephone: +45 98 90 91 50
E-mail: info.scandinavia@god.tv

ASIA & MIDDLE EAST

India
GOD TV Asia
PO Box 3455, Anna Nagar, Chennai, 600 040, India
Telephone: +91 44 2628 3737 (Toll free: 1600 44 2777)
E-mail: info.india@god.tv

Hong Kong
GOD TV Hong Kong
PO Box 35216, King's Road Post Office, Hong Kong
Telephone: (852) 3107 8877
E-mail: hongkong@god.tv

www.god.tv

You've read the ongoing miraculous story of GOD TV, but there is still much to be done...

Will you stand with us in our mammoth task of reaching one billion souls for the Kingdom of God?

The Lord has used GOD TV in redeeming the airwaves since its launch in 1995, but there is still plenty to do and we cannot do it on our own. Will you stand with Rory & Wendy and the GOD TV team as together we fulfill the Great Commission? God has used the ministry of GOD TV to achieve the impossible through media, but He also wants to fulfill His divine plans and purposes through you. Partner with us and become part of the miracle of GOD TV!

Any donation to GOD TV will be most appreciated and used for the extension of the Kingdom of God through media. Please complete the form below and fax or post to your GOD TV regional office with your check or credit card authorization. You can also make a direct deposit into GOD TV's bank account in your area (see reverse) or give online at www.god.tv

Name

Address

Tel   Email

I enclose a check for:

I authorize GOD TV to charge my credit card:

I have made a direct deposit of:

Signature: Date:

Card Expiry Date: ☐☐☐☐   Issue No: ☐☐☐☐

Please tick as applicable:

Mastercard: ☐   Maestro: ☐   American Express: ☐   Visa: ☐

Card No: ☐☐☐☐☐☐☐☐☐☐☐☐☐☐☐☐☐☐☐

Mail to: GOD TV USA, PO Box 161329 Altamonte Springs, FL 32714.
Fax: 407 862 8156. For other regional offices see www.god.tv

GOD TV BANKING DETAILS

USA BANK DETAILS

USA: BANK OF AMERICA, 3 DUPONT CIRCLE NW, WASHINGTON, D.C. 20036;
COMPANY NAME: ANGEL CHRISTIAN TELEVISION TRUST, DBA GOD TV; ACCOUNT NO:
001925993356; SWIFT CODE: BOFAUS3N; WIRE ROUTING NO: 026009593; ABA
ROUTING NO: 054001204

AUSTRALASIA BANK DETAILS

AUSTRALIA: Westpac Bank; Bank address: Parramatta Branch, CNR Church & George
STS, 264 Church Street, Parramatta NSW 2150; Account name: GOD TV;
Account number: 376610, BSB number: 032078

EUROPE BANK DETAILS

GERMANY: Deutsche Bank; Bank address: Investment & Finance Centre Hamburg –
Adolphsplatz, Adolphsplatz 7, 20457 Hamburg, Germany; Account name: Angel
Foundation; Account number: 139245500; Sort code: 200 700 00;
IBAN code: DE24 200 700 00 0139 2455 00; BIC/SWIFT Code: DEUTDEHHXXX
THE NETHERLANDS: ABN-AMRO; Bank address: Department: Corporate Non-residents
PO Box 407 (AB500) 1000 AK Amsterdam, The Netherlands; Account name: Angel
Foundation, Account number: 49 63 50 277; IBAN: NL41 ABNA 0496350277;
BIC/SWIFT code: ABNANL2A

HONG KONG BANK DETAILS

HONG KONG: HSBC; Bank address: Causeway Bay Branch; 1/F, Causeway Bay Plaza II,
463–483 Lockhart Road, Causeway Bay, Hong Kong; Account name: GOD TV;
Account number: 047–806807–001; Bank code: 004; Swift code: HSBCHKHHHKH

INDIA BANK DETAILS

For donations within India: ABN Amro Bank; Bank address: 19/1,HaddowsRoadBranch,
Nungambakkam. Chennai-600 006 India; Account name: Angel Christian Charitable
Foundation India; Account number: 780850; SWIFT code: ABNAISBBMAS;
MICR number: 600030002
Donations from outside India: The Catholic Syrian Bank; Account name: Angel Christian
Charitable Foundation India, 49, Arcot Road, Kodambakkam Chennai, India –600 024;
Account number: 20040031; SWIFT code: CSYBIN55

SCANDINAVIA BANK DETAILS

DENMARK: BG Bank; Account name: Angel Foundation; Account number: 9206 0941794;
Sort code: 9206; IBAN code: DK79 3000 000 9417 94; SWIFT code: DABADKKK
FINLAND: Bank name: Aktia Sparbank ABP; Account name: Angel Foundation; Account
number: 497028 247524; IBAN code: FI4149702820047524; SWIFT code: HELSFIHH
NORWAY: DnB NOR; Account name: Angel Foundation; Account number: 7877 08 12428;
IBAN code: NO28 7877 0812 428; SWIFT code: DNBANOKKXXX
SWEDEN: Bank name: PlusGirot; Account name: Angel Foundation; Account number: 618
5648–0; IBAN code: SE65 9500 0099 6034 6185 6480; SWIFT code: NDEASESS

UK & IRELAND BANK DETAILS

UNITED KINGDOM: Barclays Bank PLC; Bank address: Percy Street, Newcastle upon
Tyne NE1 4QL; Account name: Angel Foundation; Account number: 80757160; IBAN code:
GB80BARC20594280757160; Sort code: 20–59–42; SWIFT code: BARC GB22
GOD TV has a special account set up in the UK for those who wish to give in Euros or
Dollars
€: Barclays Bank 49755333; Sort code: 20–54–78
$: Barclays Bank 55391555; Sort code: 20–54–78

AFRICA BANK DETAILS

AFRICA: First National Bank; Bank address: 49 Main Road, Mowbray Cape Town 7705
South Africa; Account name: Angel Television Africa; Account number: 62044194025;
Branch code: 200309
For foreign donations use: BIC/Swift code FIRNZAJJ